Excel University:
Microsoft Excel® Training for CPAs and Accounting Professionals:
VOLUME 1

A walk-through of the Excel® features, functions and techniques that improve the productivity of accountants. Featuring Excel® 2013 for Windows®.

During his live CPE training sessions, Jeff Lenning CPA CITP has shown thousands of CPAs and Accounting Professionals across the country how to use Excel more effectively and how to leverage Excel to improve efficiency and reduce the time it takes to complete job tasks. This series of books is a comprehensive collection of the features, functions, and techniques that are of direct benefit to accountants working in industry, public practice, consulting, or the nonprofit sector. Each book in the Excel University series includes narrative, screenshots, Excel practice files, and video content. This series uses a hands-on approach to learning, and provides practice files and exercises that demonstrate the practical application of the items presented in each chapter.

JEFF LENNING, CPA CITP
CLICK CONSULTING, INC.

Excel University – Volume 1
By: Jeff Lenning CPA CITP
Version: 2.0

All rights reserved.
Copyright © 2013 by Jeff Lenning

ISBN-10: 1482550989
EAN-13: 9781482550986

No part of this publication may be reproduced, stored in a retrieval system or transmitted in any form or by any means, electronic, mechanical, photocopying, recording, scanning or otherwise, except as permitted under Sections 107 or 108 of the 1976 United States Copyright Act, without prior written permission.

Trademarks: Click Consulting, the logo and related trade dress are trademarks or registered trademarks of Click Consulting, Inc. and/or Jeff Lenning and affiliates, in the United States, and may not be used without written permission. Microsoft, Windows and Excel are trademarks or registered trademarks of Microsoft Corporation in the United States and/or other countries. All other trademarks are the property of their respective owners. The author is not associated with any product or vendor mentioned in this book.

Limit of liability/disclaimer of warranty: the publisher and author make no representations or warranties with respect to the accuracy or completeness of the contents of this work and specifically disclaim all warranties, including without limitation warranties of fitness for a particular purpose. No warranty may be created or extended by sales or promotional materials. The advice and strategies contained herein may not be suitable for every situation. This work is sold with the understanding that the publisher and author are not engaged in rendering legal, accounting, or other professional services. If professional assistance is required, the services of a competent professional person should be sought. Neither the publisher nor the author shall be liable for damages arising herefrom. The fact that an organization or website is referred to in this work as a citation and/or a potential source of further information does not mean that the author or the publisher endorses the information the organization or website may provide or recommendations it may make. Further, readers should be aware that internet websites listed in this work may have changed or disappeared between when this work was written and when it is read.

About the Author

In his live CPE training sessions, Jeff Lenning CPA CITP has shown thousands of CPAs and accounting professionals across the country how to use Excel to streamline their work and become more efficient. His Excel articles have been featured in several publications, including the *Journal of Accountancy* and *California CPA Magazine*. He is the founder of Click Consulting, Inc., a firm that specializes in Excel training, consulting, development, and personal coaching. Jeff graduated from the University of Southern California.

Contents at a Glance

Opening Information 15
    Chapter 1: Overview 17
    Chapter 2: Book Conventions 23
    Chapter 3: Excel Conventions 25
    Chapter 4: How to Make the Most 31

Foundations 37
    Chapter 5: Foundations Overview 39
    Chapter 6: Selected Shortcuts 41
    Chapter 7: Named References 51
    Chapter 8: Tables 65
    Chapter 9: Data Validation 77
    Chapter 10: Conditional Formatting Basics 97
    Chapter 11: Better Summing 109
    Chapter 12: Skinny Row 121
    Chapter 13: Hide Worksheets 131
    Chapter 14: Highlight Input Cells 137
    Chapter 15: Workbook Organization 145
    Chapter 16: Worksheet Organization 161
    Chapter 17: Nested Functions 179
    Chapter 18: Selection Groups 185
    Chapter 19: Workbook Design Principles 193

Conclusion 199

Table of Contents

Opening Information 15

  Chapter 1: Overview 17
    Why I Wrote the Excel University Series. 17
    About You. 17
    About Me 18
    Organization 18
    Recurring Processes 19
    Automation Snowball 20
    Continuing Education Credit. 22
    Skill Sets 22
    How Did I Pick the Content? 22

  Chapter 2: Book Conventions. 23
    References 23
    Formulas 24
    Chapter Structure. 24
    Corrections and Suggestions. 24
    Success Stories 24

  Chapter 3: Excel Conventions 25
    Terminology. 25
      Worksheets and Workbooks 25
      Features and Functions 25
      Returns 26
      Arguments 26
      Cell References 27
        Absolute and Relative References 27
        External References. 28
        Column and Row References 29

Stored Values and Displayed Values	29
Ribbons and Menus	30
Administrators and Users	30
Excel Versions	30

Chapter 4: How to Make the Most ... 31
- Overall ... 31
- Workbook Download ... 31
  - Answers Version ... 32
  - Extra Credit ... 32
  - Cells ... 32
- Reinforcement ... 33
- My Favorites ... 33

Foundations ... 37

Chapter 5: Foundations Overview ... 39

Chapter 6: Selected Shortcuts ... 41
- Arrow Keys ... 43
  - Ctrl ... 43
  - Shift ... 43
  - Ctrl + Shift ... 43
  - Function Arguments ... 44
- F2 ... 45
- F4 ... 46
- Double-Click ... 47
- Ctrl Page Up/ Page Down ... 50
- Chapter Conclusion ... 50

Chapter 7: Named References ... 51
- Set Up ... 51
- How To ... 52
- Examples ... 54
  - Name a Cell Quickly ... 54
  - Name a Range Quickly ... 56
  - Navigate ... 58
  - Name Manager ... 60

New Name	61
Change a Name	62
Delete a Name	63
Chapter Conclusion	63

Chapter 8: Tables 65
- **Set Up** 65
- **How To** 66
- **Examples** 67
  - Table Name 67
  - Auto-Expansion 69
  - Structured References 71
  - Automatic Fill-Down 72
  - Automatic Totals 73
  - Column Label Replacement 74
  - Other Ribbon Settings 75
- **Chapter Conclusion** 76
- **Additional Resources** 76

Chapter 9: Data Validation 77
- **Set Up** 77
- **How To** 79
- **Practice** 81
  - Decimal 81
  - Whole Number 83
  - List on Same Sheet 85
  - List on Different Sheet 88
  - List with Named Reference 89
  - List with Table 92
- **Chapter Conclusion** 96

Chapter 10: Conditional Formatting Basics 97
- **Set Up** 97
- **How To** 98
- **Examples** 99
  - Greater Than / Less Than 99
  - Equal To / Not Equal To 101

   Don't Use Conditional Formatting … 102
   Set up a New Rule … 103
   Apply Two Additional Rules … 103
  Duplicate Values … 104
  Data Bars … 105
  Icon Sets … 106
 Chapter Conclusion … 107

Chapter 11: Better Summing … 109
 Set Up … 109
 How To … 110
 Examples … 113
  Balance Sheet … 113
  Department Report … 116
  SG&A … 117
 Chapter Conclusion … 118
 Additional Resources … 119

Chapter 12: Skinny Row … 121
 Set Up … 121
 How To … 122
 Examples … 124
  Customer Sales … 124
  Department Report … 126
  End of Data Regions … 127
  Skinny Columns … 128
 Chapter Conclusion … 129

Chapter 13: Hide Worksheets … 131
 Set Up … 131
 How To … 132
  How to Unhide … 133
 Examples … 134
 Chapter Conclusion … 135

Chapter 14: Highlight Input Cells … 137
 Set Up … 137
 How To … 138

  Examples 140
    Monthly Payment 141
    Journal Entry 142
    Reporting 142
    With Data Validation 143
  Chapter Conclusion 143

Chapter 15: Workbook Organization 145
  Set Up 145
  How To 146
    Name All Sheets 146
    No Extra Sheets 147
    Start Here 147
      Title 148
      Company 148
      Purpose 148
      Settings 148
      Instructions 148
      Assumptions 149
      Support 149
    ErrorCk 149
    Admin 151
    Match Data Flow 151
    Color Code 152
    Print Order 152
    Index 152
  Example 153
    Start Here Worksheet 153
    ErrorCk Worksheet 156
    QBData Worksheet 157
      A Note about Importing Data 158
    Report Worksheet 159
  Chapter Conclusion 160

Chapter 16: Worksheet Organization 161
  Set Up 161
  How To 161

    Split Data from Report Sheets 164
    Flat Data 164
    Clean Data 166
    Uniform Data 166
    Accommodate Minor Structure Changes 167
    As It Comes 167
    Subtotals Outside 167
    Subtotals Above 168
    Consistent Formulas in a Region 168
    Sheet Title 168
    Company Name 169
    Column A for Labels; Begin Data in Column B 169
    Sheet Names Short but Descriptive 169
    Prefer Lookups to Direct Cell References 170
    No Blank Columns 170
    Consistent Headers 171
  Examples 171
    Flat 172
    Clean 172
    Uniform 173
    Split 174
    Subtotals Outside 174
    Subtotals Above 175
    Consistent 176
    Column A 176
  Chapter Conclusion 177

Chapter 17: Nested Functions 179
  Set Up 179
  How To 180
  Examples 181
    Balance Sheet 182
    Commission Summary 182
    Commission Detail 183
  Chapter Conclusion 184

Chapter 18: Selection Groups 185
Set Up 185
How To 185
Cells 186
Nonadjacent Cells 186
Cells and Formulas 186
Ranges 187
Sheets 187
Examples 188
Cells 188
Cell Formulas 189
Ranges 189
Sheets - Edit 191
Sheets - Delete 192
Chapter Conclusion 192

Chapter 19: Workbook Design Principles 193
Automation 194
Bulletproof 194
Check for Errors 194
Design 195
Efficiency 196
Minimize Input Cells 196
Beautiful Formulas 196
One Place 197
Efficient Use 197
Chapter Conclusion 198

Conclusion 199

OPENING INFORMATION

*Excel is my favorite computer application of all time.
My goal is to help you maximize its power.*

Chapter 1: Overview

WHY I WROTE THE EXCEL UNIVERSITY SERIES

I developed the Excel University series to provide a comprehensive collection of the features, functions, and techniques that offer the most benefit to CPAs and accounting professionals. In my live CPE training sessions, I've been fortunate to help thousands of CPAs leverage the power of Excel. I've witnessed their joy and excitement as certain features and functions are presented. I wrote this series of books to help more people leverage the power of Excel. I wrote it to reach the people who I won't have the opportunity to meet in one of my CPE sessions. I wrote it to help you.

ABOUT YOU

If you are reading this book, chances are you work in the accounting field. Much of your work is probably done, or could be done, with Excel. It is also likely that you are overwhelmed with the amount of work you have, especially when compared to the amount of available time. You probably find that your work life encroaches on your personal life, which creates anxiety. Your two worlds are colliding, and you are caught in the middle and stressed out. I know, because I was there.

The good news is that this situation doesn't have to persist. Without hiring any additional staff, and without working any harder, you can get your work done in a fraction of the time it takes you right now, just by using Excel. You will soon see how to delegate many of the mechanical tasks you perform manually to the fastest, most accurate, and most efficient worker that I know—Microsoft Excel.

ABOUT ME

I've held four positions during my career as a CPA: an auditor in public accounting, a financial analyst in industry, an accounting manager at a public company, and a consultant. In each of these roles, I learned a variety of Excel features, functions, approaches, and techniques that enabled me to get my tasks done more quickly. The most dramatic example occurred when I was an accounting manager; I was able to streamline our monthly close, reducing it from about two weeks to two days. I obtained this efficiency by delegating mechanical tasks to Excel. Blown away by the power of Excel, I decided to tell others about it. So, in 2000 I began to share what I had discovered.

It started with an article that I submitted to the *Journal of Accountancy*. It highlighted a simple Excel feature: hyperlinks. The article was eventually named "Financial Reports in a Snap" and was published in April 2000. Since then I've tried my best to show others how to save time by approaching their workbooks with proper design, technique, and the correct Excel features and functions. Fortunately, I am able to show accountants how to use Excel more effectively by providing training sessions to corporations and live CPE seminars to individual CPAs through the AICPA and the California CPA Education Foundation. While those sessions are successful, they do present constraints, namely time constraints. Typically a session is 8 hours, and that just isn't enough time to cover everything. So the Excel University series represents a comprehensive catalog of everything that I think is useful to accounting professionals. If you and I sat down together, and you asked me to tell you everything you need to know about Excel, this series of books would be my answer.

The goal of Excel University is to allow you to perform your job tasks in a fraction of the time they currently take. Excel has been my secret weapon for years, and I hope it can be yours as well. May the force be with you, my friend.

ORGANIZATION

Due to the volume of content, the Excel University series is split across several books. They should be read in a sequential order, as each book provides additional building blocks of knowledge. The series presents content in the following structure:

- First, I cover the features, functions, and techniques that I use all the time—those that I think are useful to all accountants regardless of the type of work they do.

- Next, I explore additional features and functions, while also revisiting and expanding on items covered previously.

- Toward the end of the series, I review many advanced topics and sophisticated automation techniques. These generally require a level of proficiency with Excel.

If you work through the entire series and complete all of the exercises, you'll be able to do all of your Excel tasks faster. You'll be an Excel expert. Your appreciation and love for Excel will grow. Plus, you'll probably be better looking.

RECURRING PROCESSES

Many people believe that Excel is useful to accountants because accountants are number crunchers, and there is no better tool than Excel for crunching numbers and counting beans. However, number crunching is only a small part of Excel's true utility for accountants. The true source of Excel's power for us lies in the fact that much of our work is recurring. That is, we repeat the same process or procedure each day, week, month, or quarter. Thus, when we use Excel correctly, and use the proper approaches, techniques, features, and functions, we can perform a mechanical recurring task in as little as zero time.

The Excel University series demonstrates the features and functions that enable you to use Excel in ways that you never thought possible. However, much of the content is dedicated to illustrating the features and functions that enable you to automate nearly any data-driven mechanical task, whether fully or partially. There is no substitute for human judgment, review, and thoughtfulness in your work, but if a task is purely mechanical, chances are better than not that you'll be able to automate it.

Examples of mechanical data-driven tasks that can be automated include:

- List comparisons: This happens when we compare two lists to find out if an item on one list appears on another list, such as when we try to figure out if a check has cleared the bank. To do this, we look at our check register and manually try to locate the particular check on the list of cleared checks. With the correct formula, Excel can do this task in about a millisecond. So, we'll delegate that mechanical task to Excel from now on.

- Lookups: We spend time looking up the related value from a list. For example, we have a report that shows the department ID but not the name. So we look up the name and type it into a cell. Or we have an account number but not the name, so we look up the account name. Or the customer ID, the Vendor ID, the Project ID, and, well, you get the idea. With the right function, Excel can perform that same lookup in a millisecond, so let's delegate lookups to Excel from now on.

- Reformatting reports: Many accounting applications provide certain canned reports very well, but sometimes a report that you need just doesn't exist. So to create such a report you export data to Excel and then spend a bunch of manual effort formatting it. Sometimes the formatting is simple, such as removing blank columns or updating account names. At other times, however, the formatting is more significant. For example, you may need to combine several rows into a single row, and in many cases, this type of work can be accomplished instantly by using the right Excel functions.

We'll explore many other examples and illustrations during this series.

Take a moment to add up the time you spend on these types of tasks each week. Is it an hour per week? Two hours per week? Ten? Excluding busy season, an average workweek is 40 hours. If you spend an average of four hours per week on these types of tasks, then 10% of your time is spent working on items that could easily be delegated to Excel. Since there are only 40 hours in a workweek, it is easy for people to spend a large percentage of their time doing things that can be automated with Excel; conversely, it is pretty easy to save a large percentage of a workweek by using Excel properly.

AUTOMATION SNOWBALL

Total automation is my goal. Doing things in a fraction of the time it takes other people is a passion of mine, even in my personal life. Have you been to Disney's California Adventure? The popular attraction "Soaring over California" always has about an hour's wait—unless you know the secret. If you walk up to the ride's cast member and ask for a Single Rider Pass, you'll be handed a blue ticket that almost seems to glow. With this ticket in hand, you can walk past everyone else to the front of the line and hop on the very next ride. The adrenaline rush I get from walking past a one-hour line is far better than the rush I get from the ride itself. If you know the secret, or the trick, you can enjoy the attraction in a fraction of the time it takes other people, and I just love that. In this spirit, I can't wait to show you all of the time-saving tricks waiting for you in Excel.

Have you heard of the 'debt snowball' principle referred to by top financial experts? In summary, you pay off your lowest balance first and then use that payment to attack the next largest balance, and so on. This process creates a snowball effect that gains momentum once it gets going. I view Excel automation in much the same way, and thus, I call it the automation snowball.

The automation snowball starts in the first month by investing time to automate a single recurring task or process. The next month, you use the time you saved in the first month to automate another task. The following month, you automate another task. The cumulative effect adds up to some serious time savings. I know, because this was the approach I used, and it worked.

I was overwhelmed by the amount of work I had to get done in the little time I had available. I also viewed Excel simply as a tool to perform calculations quickly. But as I explored the program's features and functions, I began to view Excel as a platform that could automate virtually any mechanical, recurring, data-driven task. So each month I focused on delegating one task to Excel. Sometimes automating that task took just a little bit of time, and sometimes it required substantial effort to figure out the formulas. But in all cases, my time investment paid handsome efficiency dividends. I easily recaptured the initial time invested, because I enjoyed significant time-savings each subsequent period. I continuously looked for tasks to delegate to Excel. No matter how small a task was or how little time it would take to perform manually, if it could be automated, it was automated. The automation of various large and small manual tasks added up to a considerable amount of work being handled by Excel. After delegating mechanical tasks to Excel and focusing on the automation snowball, I began to have time to breath. My job became more enjoyable and far less stressful.

In my live presentations, I'm often asked how I found time to dedicate to process improvement. Typically the people who ask me this question are inundated with work. For them, imagining a day when they have enough time to invest in process improvement seems far off. In the wise words of The Merovingian, "… but if we do not ever take time, how can we ever have time?" The exciting truth of the matter is that I only had to take time the first couple of months; after that, my workload decreased because of the automation, and I found that I had plenty of time to dedicate to process improvement.

If you are going to embark on an adventure of automating your tasks with Excel, keep in mind that no task is too small. Start with the big ones first, of course, and get some of that low-hanging fruit. But bear in mind that even small manual processes should eventually be automated. It is natural to underestimate the value of shaving off only a minute from a recurring task. But remember that the total time saved is calculated by multiplying the savings of each cycle by the number of cycles. When you add up the savings of all your recurring tasks, including those that recur annually, quarterly, monthly, weekly, and daily, even small savings add up. And so far we're just talking about savings for you—just one person in your company. When you have many employees working to automate tasks, the impact is magnified. That is why I don't hesitate to take the time to eliminate even a single minute from a recurring process.

Am I overselling the efficiency gains? The potential productivity gain depends on the kind of work you do. If you mostly work on one-time workbooks and much of your day is spent in front of clients and not in front of Excel, then you probably will not achieve huge efficiency gains. However, if you are the person in your firm or company doing recurring Excel work, then you'll definitely be able to realize significant efficiency gains. Generally, the people who spend their days crunching numbers, generating reports, and performing analyses are the people with the most to gain from this course.

Much of the discussion above is focused on recurring processes. Even if your job tasks do not recur and you generally build workbooks that are used only one time, you'll still find plenty of content in this course to help make those workbooks more efficient and bulletproof.

CONTINUING EDUCATION CREDIT

My company is not NASBA certified, and thus my firm can't provide CPE for this course. If you are looking for CPE credit, please feel free to refer to the AICPA or CalCPA websites. Search for courses authored by Jeff Lenning, and you'll be able to pick up CPE credit for my Excel self-study products or live sessions.

SKILL SETS

I didn't write this series of books with any given skill set in mind, but instead I wrote it with the accountant in mind. Topics range from beginning to advanced. I've tried my best to present content in the correct order, so that by starting at the beginning and following along in progression, all readers should be fine, regardless of their previous Excel experience.

While most of the content should be useful to you, some may not; it just depends on the type of work you do. Feel free to pick and choose and don't get stuck in the details of an item you won't use or that is too hard right now … just skip it and revisit it in the future if needed.

HOW DID I PICK THE CONTENT?

Excel is a big program, and Microsoft has done a great job of including numerous features and functions that are helpful to many different disciplines. The content of this course really focuses on the features and functions useful to accounting professionals.

I've selected the features and functions that I've used during my CPA career and have focused on those items that have saved time. I've designed the content to be useful to accountants, and I sincerely hope it is useful to you.

Chapter 2: Book Conventions

This chapter discusses the conventions used throughout the Excel University series.

REFERENCES

When determining the order in which to present content, I carefully considered many factors. One of my goals was to introduce features and functions in the order in which they build upon each other. I tried to introduce an item only after prerequisite items were introduced. To better track and organize topics during my planning process, I set up dependency notes for each topic. These notes helped to ensure that topics were presented in the proper order.

I've included the dependency notes in the text, as well as a handful of other helpful references. Following are the types of references you'll encounter throughout the text:

DEPENDS ON – The item being presented depends on an item previously presented.

XREF – A cross reference to a related or complimentary item.

NOTE – A general note about the item being presented.

KB – The keyboard shortcut or shortcuts used to perform the task.

PRACTICE – A reference to the exercise workbook and worksheet.

VIDEO – The URL link to the related video content.

FORMULAS

Formulas are presented in monospaced font, as follows:

`=SUM(A1:A10)`

Any additional information about the formula or function is explained immediately after the formula.

CHAPTER STRUCTURE

In general, I have organized each chapter with the following structure:

- Set Up – Provides an overview and highlights the benefits and uses.
- How To – Details how to implement the feature or function.
- Examples – Suggest hands-on exercises that illustrate an application of the feature or function.

CORRECTIONS AND SUGGESTIONS

If you find any errors in the book or the exercise workbooks, please, PLEASE, let me know so that I can correct them in the next revision. Send a note to info@clickconsulting.com.

Also, if you have any suggestions for content, additional application of presented features or functions, or anything else that you think should be incorporated into this text, please let me know.

SUCCESS STORIES

I love to hear success stories, which make me all warm and fuzzy inside and provide me with inspiration and motivation. Please take a moment to share your process improvements, especially those tasks that now take less time. Drop a note to info@clickconsulting.com.

Chapter 3: Excel Conventions

This chapter discusses a variety of Excel terms and references that we'll use throughout the Excel University series.

TERMINOLOGY

Let's start by covering some Excel-specific terminology. Getting these terms cleared up now will provide a better experience during the remainder of this text.

WORKSHEETS AND WORKBOOKS

A *workbook* is the file that you open with Excel. There are typically many *worksheets* in a single workbook, and they are represented as tabs at the bottom of the Excel window.

FEATURES AND FUNCTIONS

Throughout this book, I'll use the term *function* to describe an Excel worksheet function. An example of this is the SUM function. Functions will be denoted in this text in uppercase, like SUM or SUMIF. I'll use the term *feature* to describe a feature of Excel that you will use by interacting with menus, ribbons, icons, and buttons, such as the PivotTable feature.

RETURNS

A function *returns* a value to a cell. For example, the SUM function returns a sum to the cell. So, when I use the word *returns*, you'll know that I am referring to the function's result.

ARGUMENTS

Most Excel worksheet functions use *arguments* to compute results. Function arguments are the cell references, values, and functions that are placed within parentheses following the function's name, such as the SUM function below:

`=SUM(A1:A10)`

This function has one function argument: the range A1:A10.

Some Excel functions have many function arguments. Consider the payment function below:

`=PMT(rate, nper, pv, [fv], [type])`

The PMT function is used to compute the payment of a loan and has five function arguments. You'll notice that two of these arguments are enclosed in square brackets, specifically [fv] and [type]. Function arguments enclosed in square brackets in this text, and inside of Excel, are optional. Optional arguments do not need to be expressed specifically inside the function. When an optional argument is omitted, it assumes a default value. So, consider the PMT function below:

`=PMT(.02,36,1000)`

Only the first three arguments are specified. Since the two optional arguments are omitted, their default values are used in the calculation. In this case, the default values are fv=0 and type=0.

 **KB**

A quick way to enter formulas is to use auto-complete. After you enter an equal sign in the cell and begin typing the first few letters of a function name, you'll notice that Excel displays the auto-complete box. You can use your keyboard Arrow keys to select the desired function, and then press the Tab key to insert it into the cell.

CELL REFERENCES

While we are at it, we may as well make sure we are all on the same page with regard to syntax for absolute and relative cell and range references.

Absolute and Relative References

Excel automatically updates *relative* cell references as the formula is filled or copied to other cells. When you use a relative cell reference in a formula, you ask Excel to refer to a cell relative to the formula cell (e.g., cell to the left). Excel preserves the relative nature of the reference by automatically updating it as you fill or copy the formula to other cells. Relative cell references contain row and column labels only, such as A1 or B10. For example, after writing the formula =A1*2 in cell B1 and then filling the formula down to B2, you'll notice that Excel updates the cell reference in the formula to =A2*2, thus preserving the relative nature of the reference.

Excel does not update *absolute* cell references as the formula is filled or copied to other cells. When you use an absolute cell reference, you ask Excel to refer to a fixed cell location on the worksheet, regardless of the location of the formula cell. Excel preserves the fixed cell reference and does not update it as you fill or copy the formula to other cells. Absolute cell references contain dollar signs in front of the row and column labels, such as A1 or B10. When you insert the dollar signs, you essentially lock down the row and column labels. Absolute cell references like A1 or B10 will not be updated as you fill or copy the formula to other cells.

A *mixed* cell reference uses a relative reference and an absolute reference at the same time. For example, $A1 is a cell reference that has an absolute column reference and a relative row reference, while A$1 has a relative column reference with an absolute row reference. The relative portion of the cell reference will be updated as the formula is filled or copied, whereas the absolute portion will be unchanged. The dollar sign in the cell reference $A1 locks down the column reference (A) so that Excel will not update the column reference as the formula is filled or copied left or right. The dollar sign in the cell reference B$10 locks down the row reference (10) so that Excel will not update the row reference as the formula is filled or copied up or down.

When I use Excel, I try my best to write formulas that will continue to work when filled or copied to other cells. The key is to use the proper cell references (absolute, relative, or mixed). During this course, feel free to think through the type of references you will require so that as you fill a formula down or to the right, it will work as intended.

External References

In addition to understanding the difference between absolute and relative cell references, it is useful to be aware of the syntax for referencing a cell on a different worksheet. In general, we don't need to write the reference as we build the formula, since Excel kindly enters it for us when we click the cell. However, understanding Excel's syntax will help as we dig into some of the more advanced content.

To refer to a cell on a different sheet, use the sheet name, an exclamation mark, and then the cell reference. If the sheet name has a space in it, you'll need to surround the sheet name with single apostrophes. For example, to reference cell A1 in a sheet named Sheet1 use:

```
=Sheet1!A1
```

To reference cell A1 in a sheet named My Worksheet use:

```
='My Worksheet'!A1
```

If a sheet name has no spaces in it, you can still surround the sheet name with single apostrophes:

```
='Sheet1'!A1
```

If the cell is on the same sheet as the formula, you can either include or exclude the sheet name from the reference. In practice, the sheet name is typically excluded when the cell is on the same sheet as the formula.

How do we reference a cell in a different workbook? Well, honestly, we do everything possible to avoid that, as it's not a good idea to reference cells in other workbooks. Preferably, we combine the workbooks into a single workbook, so that all cell references are internal or within the same workbook. However, if the need arises to refer to a cell in a different workbook, the syntax includes the workbook path, workbook name in square brackets, sheet name, exclamation mark, and cell reference, as follows:

```
='c:\jeff\files\[sample.xlsx]My Worksheet'!A1
```

Excel usually enters the appropriate syntax, so you probably won't need to memorize it, but it's good to understand how the syntax works.

 **NOTE**

> When referencing cells in other workbooks, it is a good idea to use a Named Reference, rather than a row/column cell reference. The structure of the external file can then change without breaking your reference and formula results.

Named References are discussed in Chapter 7.

Column and Row References

To wrap up our reference discussion, let's review column and row references. As you already know, you can write a function to sum a range:

=SUM(A1:A100)

You can tweak that formula to sum all of the cells in the column:

=SUM(A:A)

By excluding row references, and just using the column letters (e.g., A:A or B:B), you create column-only references. Functions that use column references include all data in the column, including new data subsequently entered into the column.

The same thing works for row references. For example, to sum up all columns in row 10:

=SUM(10:10)

STORED VALUES AND DISPLAYED VALUES

Throughout this text, when I refer to a cell's *stored value,* I am referring to the value that the user enters into the cell: the value that is being stored in the cell. Sometimes I simply use the term *value* to mean *stored value*. In addition to stored values, cells also have *displayed values*. A displayed value is the value that the user sees when looking at a cell. Stored values and displayed values differ due to cell formatting. For example, a cell's stored value may be 12345.67, while the cell's displayed value may be $12,345.67. Being able to realize and articulate this difference will help as we work through certain features and functions.

As a general rule, worksheet functions operate on the cell's stored value and not on the cell's displayed value. This will be important to remember when we explore text and lookup functions.

RIBBONS AND MENUS

As you recall, Excel users experienced a brutal re-learning curve when moving from Excel 2003 to Excel 2007. The Microsoft developers switched everything around and removed our Menus, replacing them with Ribbons. Thus, throughout this text, I've referred to navigation through the Ribbon interface as follows:

- RibbonUI: Ribbon Tab Name > Button Name

I've referred to the navigation in Menu-driven versions of Excel (Excel 2003 and earlier) as follows:

- MenuUI: Menu Name > Menu Item > Sub Menu Item

ADMINISTRATORS AND USERS

Throughout this text, I reference workbook *administrator* and workbook *user*, a distinction that is sometimes important. I use the term administrator to refer to the person who initially develops the workbook. Think of the administrator as the architect or designer. I use the term user to refer to the person who is responsible for entering data into the workbook or otherwise performing ongoing maintenance.

EXCEL VERSIONS

The screenshots in this series were captured with Microsoft Excel 2013 for Windows. For the most part, I note in the text how to navigate to the feature using the Ribbon and Button names. Not all features discussed in this text are available in older versions of Excel. When possible, I note how to navigate to the feature in older versions of Excel by using the Menu and Menu Item names. Additionally, not all features presented in this text are available in Excel for Mac.

Chapter 4: How to Make the Most

Here are my thoughts about how to make the most of our time together and how to maximize the benefits of working through the Excel University series.

OVERALL

Your current skill level and goals dictate the best way to work through the content.

If you are already skilled at using Excel and your goal is to simply pick up some new tips and tricks, then I suggest that you skip through the content and look for items or applications that are new to you. You may immediately see how these items are applicable to your work. If you'd like to play along, feel free to practice with the workbooks that are provided.

If your goal is to maximize the benefit of this series, and you want to transform the way you use Excel, then I suggest going through the content sequentially, methodically, and slowly. I recommend working through all practice exercises, because nothing is a substitute for hands-on work. Reference the video content if you need extra insight or help. This process takes longer, but the end result is that you'll be an Excel ninja, capable of doing things faster and more precisely than ever before.

WORKBOOK DOWNLOAD

In my opinion, the best way to learn Excel is by hands-on experience, and I have provided sample Excel workbooks that you can use to practice. Each workbook has a worksheet named Start Here, which identifies the topic presented and lists each exercise and its purpose. The exercise sheets are incomplete. You complete the exercise by writing a formula or function or by using a feature. These workbooks aren't provided as a reference, rather, they are designed for you to work through and complete.

The exercises attempt to demonstrate the application of each feature and function in a relevant and practical way.

Please feel free to download the workbooks from the following:

- www.clickconsulting.com/books

The download is a single Zip file containing all of the Excel files. Extract the Zip file to gain access to the practice files.

ANSWERS VERSION

You'll notice that there are essentially two versions of each workbook.

- The exercise version is referenced by name in this text. It provides space to write the formulas and otherwise complete various exercises included in the workbook.

- The answers version is denoted with _answers appended to the file name. It contains the completed exercises and formulas.

EXTRA CREDIT

Some exercise workbooks have Extra Credit worksheets. As a rule, the sheets named Exercise are demonstrated in this text. The Extra Credit worksheets carry the feature beyond what is presented in this text, providing additional examples and illustrations. The answers for the Extra Credit exercises are included in the answers version of each workbook.

CELLS

Inside the exercise worksheets, the built-in cell style Output is used to identify the cells that require your formula or function. The Output cell style has bold text, with a thin black cell outline and a pale gray fill.

REINFORCEMENT

This series attempts to reinforce topics throughout the content. For example, you'll notice that we first cover a feature or a function at a basic level and later revisit the item and explain advanced uses or attributes, or show how to use the feature in conjunction with a complimentary feature or function. This strategy helps to reinforce the item over time, and, more importantly, allows us to increase the complexity, and thus usefulness, of each item.

I've heard that people learn more effectively when they can tie new information to something they already know. If that is true, then trying to connect a new feature or function to your existing workbooks will help reinforce the item. Take a moment to mentally scan through your existing workbooks and see if the new feature or function can improve them. Conversely, if you discover a new feature, but don't see how it will ever apply to the work you are doing, simply make a note of the capabilities and then move along. If you encounter a workbook in the future where the feature may apply, you can dig in and work through the details as needed.

Probably the most effective way to reinforce what you've learned is to use the practice workbooks. All of the examples and screenshots presented in the book are also presented in the workbooks, so you can play along. My personal learning style is hands-on, so I spent time preparing the exercise files for you. I encourage you to use them!

MY FAVORITES

As you progress through this series, it may be helpful to make a list of the items that are the most relevant to you and that you want to implement into your workbooks. Feel free to make notes of those items in the My Favorites table that follows.

MY FAVORITES

Feel free to make a note of features or functions that you want to remember to practice and implement into your workbooks as you work through the content.

PAGE	TOPIC

PAGE	TOPIC

FOUNDATIONS

Building a great workbook requires a solid foundation.

Chapter 5: Foundations Overview

This section of the Excel University series is called Foundations because the features, functions, and techniques covered represent the fundamental building blocks required to build powerful workbooks.

This section sets the foundation for future learning and ensures that as we work through more sophisticated items, all readers will understand the content and be able to successfully implement the ideas presented.

Chapter 6: Selected Shortcuts

As I stated earlier, I like to do things in less time than other people. I like efficiency. I like automation. I like tricks, shortcuts, macros, and anything else that helps me reduce the time it takes to perform a given task or business process.

While it may seem contradictory, the concepts of *faster* and *better* are not opposites. Increasing speed does not mean decreasing quality. In fact, when I automate a business process with Excel, the result is typically more accurate than the former process. That is, efficiency and accuracy generally increase simultaneously when the Excel solution is applied.

I like to break efficiency gains into two distinct categories, process efficiency and personal productivity.

Process efficiency is improving the efficiency of a process or task. This is accomplished by automating manual steps or by otherwise using Excel's features and functions to decrease the time it takes to complete a task. For example, let's say you used to spend two hours each week preparing a report, but by using Excel's PivotTable feature, you reduce the time to two minutes each week.

Personal productivity is improving the speed with which you use Excel. This is accomplished by decreasing the time it takes you to perform an Excel command. For example, let's say you normally spend 10 seconds filling a formula down through 5,000 rows, but by using a built-in Excel shortcut, you reduce that time to one second.

I like to think of this second type of efficiency, personal productivity, as how fast I can communicate with the software and tell it what to do. With faster communication I can dramatically improve my personal productivity, and the best way to communicate quickly with Excel is to use keyboard shortcuts.

Generally, you'll be able to complete any given Excel command more quickly with a keyboard than a mouse. There are exceptions, and certain tasks are done more efficiently with a mouse, such as selecting nonadjacent ranges or filling formulas down in columns adjacent to data.

At first, using shortcuts may feel slow because you have to think, remember, and concentrate on each one. However, the shortcuts will gradually become so second nature that when you focus on what you want to have happen in Excel, your hands and fingers will automatically accomplish the tasks. Some refer to this as muscle memory; I refer to it as *awesome*.

Additionally, when you use keyboard commands, your enjoyment of using Excel will increase. You'll feel more in control and will be able to see your workbooks more clearly. You'll eventually stop seeing the menus, ribbons, tabs, dialog boxes, and buttons, and you'll just see your worksheet. It's almost like being Neo from *The Matrix*.

I forced myself to learn keyboard shortcuts by playing a game each morning. I would come into the office, grab a cup of coffee, and then sit down at my computer. I would time how long I could work in Excel before grabbing the mouse. In the beginning, it was only a few seconds. But I continued to figure out how to perform each task with the keyboard, and eventually, I could go for minutes, and then hours.

Don't underestimate the power of keyboard shortcuts. They'll help you perform your job more quickly.

This chapter discusses my Top 5 favorite shortcuts. We'll cover others later, but for now, please commit the following five shortcuts to memory and begin using them immediately:

1. Arrow keys
2. F2
3. F4
4. Double-click
5. Ctrl + PageUp/PageDown

PRACTICE

If you'd like to play along, please refer to Keyboard Shortcut Basics.xlsx.

VIDEO

To watch me complete the exercises, please visit the Excel University video library at www.clickconsulting.com/books.

ARROW KEYS

First, let's tackle worksheet navigation. Instead of grabbing for your mouse to move to a different cell, get in the habit of using the Arrow keys on your keyboard. Arrow keys move the active cell one cell left, right, up, or down, depending on which of the four Arrow keys you select.

PRACTICE

Practice Arrow key navigation by referring to the Exercise 1 worksheet.

I know this may seem boring or stupid right now, but hang in there with me a little longer. The Arrow keys on your keyboard move only one cell at a time, but we'll discover shortly how to add more power to them.

CTRL

Holding the control (Ctrl) key down while pressing an Arrow key will jump you to the edge of a data region. That is, if you are in a value cell and you press Ctrl+Down Arrow, you'll jump to the last row with data: the bottom edge of the current data region. If you press Ctrl+Up Arrow, you'll jump to the top edge of the data region: the first row with data.

Similarly, if you are in an empty cell and use Ctrl+Arrow, you'll jump to the edge of the first encountered data region; that is, to the first cell with data.

Using Arrow keys in conjunction with Ctrl enables you to scoot around your worksheet very efficiently and effectively. Now, let's see how to add more power to the Arrow keys.

SHIFT

Holding the Shift key down while pressing an Arrow key extends your selection one cell at a time. For example, by holding down the Shift key while pressing the down Arrow, you extend the selection of the original cell to include the cell below as well. This leaves two cells selected. The Shift key extends your selection.

CTRL + SHIFT

So far we have discussed that while using Arrow keys, the Shift key extends your selection, and the Ctrl key jumps you to the edge of a data region. If you hold down both the Ctrl key and the Shift key at the same time, you will extend your selection to the edge of a data region.

For example, let's say that the active cell is the top cell in a column of data. Press and hold both the Ctrl key and the Shift key, and then press the down Arrow key to instantly select the whole column of numbers.

If the active cell is the top left cell of a region of data, press and hold the Ctrl and Shift keys, and then press the right Arrow and then press the down Arrow to select the whole region.

> **KB**
>
> An alternative keyboard shortcut to select all cells in the region of the active cell is Ctrl+A.

FUNCTION ARGUMENTS

As discussed above, using the Arrow keys in conjunction with the Ctrl key and Shift key provides a fast way to navigate within a worksheet. In addition, when writing a formula, you can use the exact same keyboard shortcuts to select cell and range function arguments, and this technique works with any function.

Let's use a simple example. The SUM function includes an argument that identifies the range to sum. Rather than using a mouse to highlight the range to sum, and rather than manually typing the range reference, you can use the keyboard shortcuts discussed above. Consider the SUM function shown in Figure 1 below.

Figure 1

You can quickly navigate to cell E37 by using keyboard shortcuts. Next, begin the function by typing an equal sign = and the function name SUM. To define the argument, type an open parenthesis, which is the left "arm" of the parenthesis bracket pair. Now, instead of grabbing for the mouse to highlight the sum range, simply use the Arrow keys along with the Ctrl and Shift keys to highlight cells E12:E36. Last, close the function with a closing parenthesis, which is the right "arm" of the parenthesis bracket pair, and press Enter. No mouse needed!

> **NOTE**
>
> This exercise was designed to demonstrate how to set range and cell references for any function with the keyboard rather than the mouse. In the case of the SUM function specifically, there are other methods to insert it directly under a range, including the Sum button and other keyboard shortcuts (Alt+=), which we'll discuss in detail later. At this point, I just wanted to direct your attention to the fact that function arguments can be specified with the navigation shortcuts discussed above.

F2

The F2 key on your keyboard has many uses. For now, we will focus on using it to edit the formula or value in the current cell. Pressing F2 puts the active cell into edit mode and places the cursor inside the cell so it is ready for editing. Additionally, if the active cell contains a formula, F2 lights up the formula by color-coding each cell or range reference. This makes it fast and easy to visually see and identify the cells used in the formula.

> **PRACTICE**
>
> To follow along, please refer to the Exercise 2 worksheet.

I use F2 all the time to spot check my formulas and ensure that cell references are correct. Anytime I write a formula that I fill down or across, I ensure that my cell references (absolute, relative, mixed) work throughout the filled range as expected. I start with one of the formula cells and then press F2 to light up the cells. If the correct cells light up, I hit the escape key on my keyboard and then use the Arrow keys to navigate to another formula cell in the filled range. I hit F2 again and verify that the proper cells light up. I do this a few times just to ensure that I wrote the formula accurately, and made proper use of absolute, relative, or mixed references. By using F2, Escape, and Arrow keys repeatedly, I can quickly and efficiently spot-check my formulas to ensure that the range references are as expected.

When you use F2 and light up a formula, you can use the mouse to change the range reference by dragging the lighted cell outlines. For example, if you hit F2 and notice that a cell is improperly excluded from the formula, you can use your mouse to click and drag the colored outline to select the proper range.

Once you press F2, you are able to edit the cell value or formula using the keyboard. If you recall, we discussed how to use the Arrow keys and the Shift and Ctrl keys on your keyboard to navigate and select cells in a worksheet. Those same shortcuts work while editing the text in cells. Specifically, the left and right Arrow keys move one character to the left or right. The Shift key extends your selection, and the Ctrl key jumps to the previous or next word. Using Shift with Ctrl together extends your selection one word at a time. The Home key jumps to the beginning of the text, and the End key jumps to the end of the text.

> **NOTE**
>
> While editing a formula, you may notice that sometimes the Arrow keys navigate within the text of the formula and other times they navigate worksheet cells. Pressing the F2 key while editing a formula toggles the behavior.

F4

The F4 key on your keyboard has many uses. For now, we'll use the F4 key as a handy way to change a cell reference from relative to absolute to mixed. F4 toggles the cell reference through all four possible reference styles. Think of it as a fast way to enter dollar signs for absolute cell references.

> **XREF**
>
> Discussion of absolute, relative, and mixed cell/range references can be found in the Cell References section in Chapter 3.

Pressing the F4 key on the keyboard while editing a formula cycles the active cell reference through all four settings, as follows:

- Absolute reference (e.g., A1)
- Mixed reference (absolute row reference) (e.g., A$1)
- Mixed reference (absolute column reference) (e.g., $A1)
- Relative reference (e.g., A1)

So, if you were in a cell with a formula (e.g., =A1), and your cursor was either immediately in front of the cell reference (in front of the A), in between the row and column reference (between the A and the 1), or immediately after the reference (immediately after then 1), then pressing the F4 key would cycle through all four possible cell reference styles, as follows:

- A1 > A1 > A$1 > $A1 > A1 > etc.

PRACTICE

Practice the F4 shortcut by referring to the Exercise 3 worksheet.

There are a couple of subtle things we should cover at this time.

First, the cell reference that is changed when the F4 key is pressed is the one located beneath the cursor.

Second, when you enter a range reference (e.g., A1:G10) instead of a cell reference (e.g., A1), the whole range reference is updated only the first time the range is selected. So, be sure to use F4 as needed as you initially write the formula (before pressing Enter). To clarify, you'll notice that a range reference is actually comprised of two cell references separated by a colon, for example, A1:G10. If you press F4 immediately after entering the range reference for the first time, you'll update both cell references, which is good because it is fast. On the other hand, if you type the formula and press Enter, and then come back later to edit the formula, using F4 will only update one of the two cell references (rather than the entire range reference). This means that you'll either need to (1) select both cell references before pressing F4 or (2) press F4 for the first cell reference, and then again for the second cell reference. Thus, it is most efficient to use F4 as you initially write the formula.

DOUBLE-CLICK

As with just about anything in Excel, there are several different ways to achieve the same result. For example, you can use numerous techniques to fill a formula down a column. The double-click shortcut is one of the fastest ways that I know of.

To accomplish this shortcut (this is a shortcut, not a keyboard shortcut), simply double-click the lower right corner of a formula cell to push the formula down as far as there are adjacent data cells.

PRACTICE

Practice the double-click shortcut on the Exercise 4 worksheet.

For example, consider the Commission column in Figure 2 below.

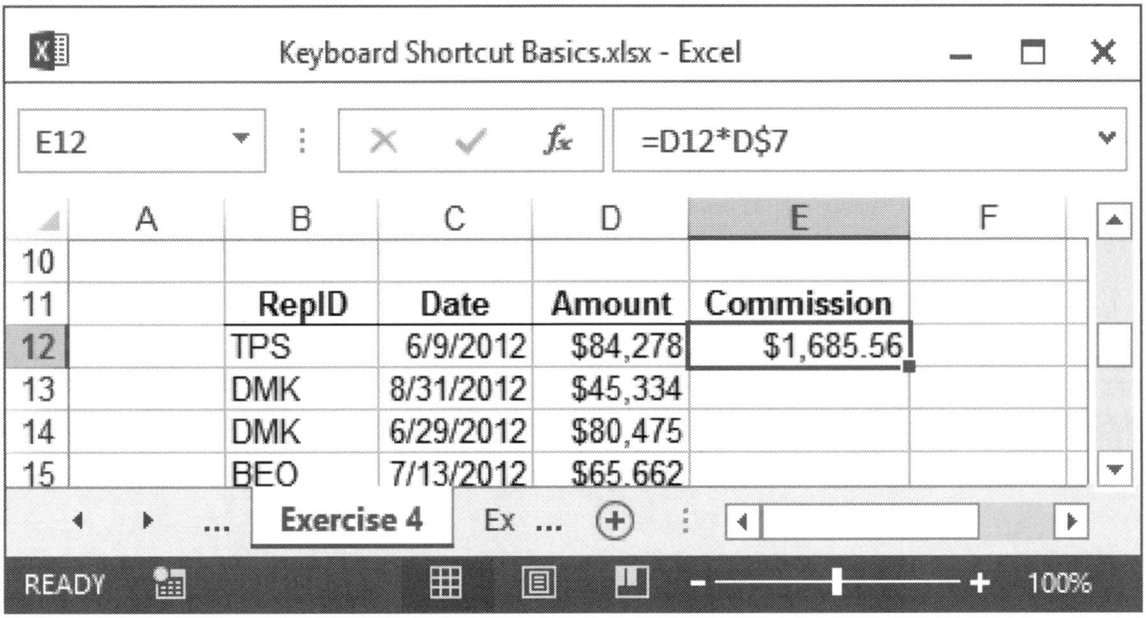

Figure 2

You can quickly push down the commission formula in E12. Start by selecting the formula cell, in this case E12. After the formula cell is activated, position the mouse to the lower-right corner of the cell until your cursor changes from a white plus to a black plus. Then, simply double-click the lower right corner of the cell to fill the formula down. The formula is filled down based on the adjacent cells containing the data. In this case, the formula is filled down through row 23, since column D has data down through row 23, as shown in Figure 3 below.

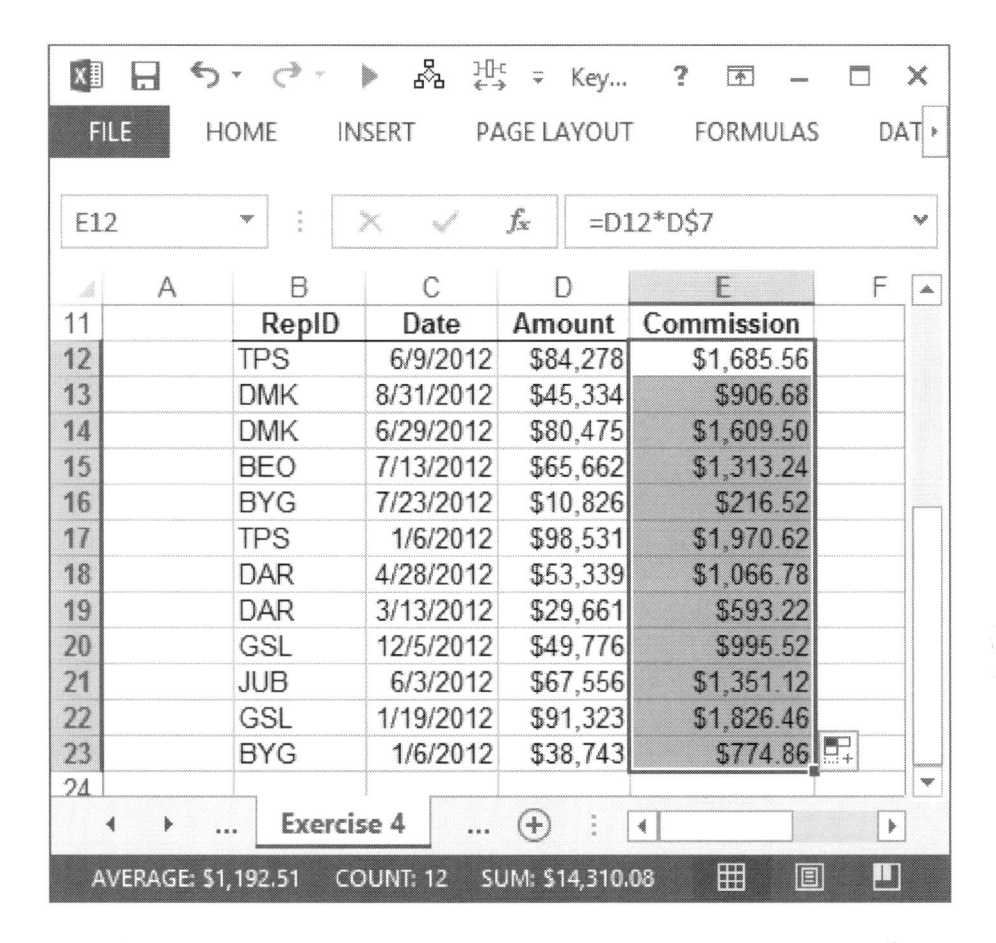

Figure 3

🛈 NOTE

You may notice that I used a mixed cell reference (D$7) instead of an absolute cell reference (D7) for the commission assumption in the formula. In this specific example, an absolute cell reference would have provided the same computational results and would have been just fine. I chose to use a mixed cell reference here for two reasons. First, I wanted to be sure to illustrate an example of a mixed cell reference since we've been talking about them. If you haven't used mixed cell references before, I wanted to be sure to demonstrate this concept early in the course. Second, I tend to lock down only the necessary part of the cell reference so that the formulas can easily be used as the worksheet is adapted and modified in the future. Since the formula is not filled left or right, locking down the column reference is not necessary.

CTRL PAGE UP/ PAGE DOWN

The last of our Top 5 favorite shortcuts shows how to switch between different worksheets within a workbook. To navigate to the previous sheet, hold down the control (Ctrl) key and then press the Page Up key. To move to the next sheet, the command is Ctrl + Page Down.

PRACTICE

Practice the Ctrl PageUp/PageDown shortcut with the Exercise 5 worksheet.

For now, focus on these five shortcuts, as they provide immediate efficiency. Later on, we'll explore additional shortcuts to help you speed along, including how to navigate the ribbon, menus, and dialog boxes.

NOTE

If you are just loving keyboard shortcuts so far and can't wait for more, here is something easy to practice: the Alt key. If you are trying to activate a Ribbon item, simply press and release the Alt key on your keyboard. Excel will then show you the keyboard letter assigned to each Ribbon tab. Press the keyboard letter to activate the Ribbon tab and reveal the shortcut letters for each individual Ribbon command button. By using this technique, you can use the keyboard to interact with the Ribbon, and you'll discover that you quickly memorize the sequence for buttons you use often. Additionally, the underlined letter of a field name in dialog boxes and elsewhere is the Alt key shortcut. For example, if you see a field or button called New, and the N is underlined, you can activate it by pressing Alt+N. Keep your eyes open as you navigate dialog boxes, ribbons, and menus, and begin to use the corresponding Alt key shortcut. Using the Alt key will help you discover how to perform many commands in Excel with your keyboard.

CHAPTER CONCLUSION

Those are my Top 5 favorite shortcuts. While I hope that you have enjoyed them, I really hope that you'll make a commitment to use them. Try to use them as you complete the exercises throughout the remainder of this book. I suspect that by the end, you won't need to think about them, and you'll be using Excel more efficiently than ever. Plus, Excel will be more fun!

Chapter 7: Named References

OK, on to our first real Excel feature … yeah! This feature is foundational to building great workbooks.

Typically, cell and range references are created using traditional row/column references, such as A1 or B1:G10, and often this approach is just fine. However, an alternative approach, known as Named References, provides numerous benefits.

SET UP

A Named Reference is a friendly name that refers to a cell, range, or other item. You define the name (e.g., commission_rate) and the underlying reference (e.g., B22). Once defined, you can use the name instead of the traditional A1 style reference. A name can be used just about anywhere Excel requires a cell or range reference, such as in formulas or macros, or as function arguments, chart sources, or PivotTable report sources.

The benefits of using names are numerous, for example:

- Easier to navigate (select the name from the Name Box to instantly navigate to the range)

- Easier to write formulas (because you don't need to navigate to a sheet and select a range)

- Easier to understand formulas (names make it easier to interpret function arguments)

- Faster to insert names into formulas with the paste name (F3) key

- Easier to define a Data Validation list source

- Easier to define the source for PivotTables and charts
- More reliable for external workbook references (won't break if the structure of the underlying workbook changes)
- Easier to refer to a name from within a macro

HOW TO

The simple way to insert a name is to highlight the cell or range, type the name in the Name Box, and then press the Enter key on your keyboard. The Name Box is the small box just to the left of the formula bar, pictured in Figure 4 below.

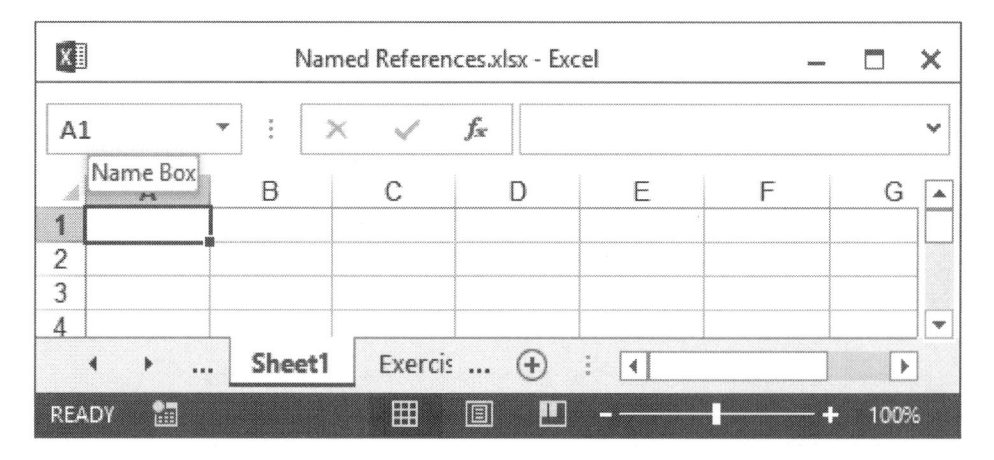

Figure 4

> **NOTE**
>
> It is important to realize that you must press the Enter key on your keyboard to set the name. If you simply type the name and then click a different cell, the name won't be registered. You must press the Enter key on your keyboard. A good way to ensure that you successfully entered the name is by examining the Name Box. The Name Box shows the name of the currently selected cell or range. If you navigate to other cells and then back to your cell, the Name Box should show your new name. If not, you may need to re-enter the name.

> **NOTE**
>
> If you enter a name into the Name Box that already exists, rather than setting the name as intended you'll simply be navigated to the reference defined by the existing name.

> **NOTE**
>
> Another quick way to ensure that you successfully entered the name is by using the pull-down arrow on the Name Box to visually ensure that your new name is listed. You can navigate to (jump to) a name by using the pull down menu to select the name or by typing the name into the Name Box. You'll be taken to the underlying reference. This is a great technique for quickly navigating to names throughout your workbooks.

> **KB**
>
> Use the F5 (GoTo) key to jump to names in your workbook.

Alternatively, you can enter a new name, as well as edit or delete an existing name, by activating the Name Manager via the following:

- RibbonUI: Formulas > Name Manager
- MenuUI: Insert > Name > Define

Once you have defined a name for a cell or a range, you can refer to that cell or range in formulas or functions by using the name.

> **NOTE**
>
> A worksheet can have any number of names that refer to a specific cell or range. While this is flexible, it can lead to confusion. Don't be confused then when you see a name in the Name Box that you are not expecting. It probably means that there is an additional name referring to the active cell. To delete old, unnecessary, or duplicate names, simply use the Name Manager. The Name Manager is also how you edit the name or the reference of any name.

NOTE

There are limitations on the names you can use. Names can't contain spaces, begin with a number or funky character, or conflict with any built-in reference. For example, you can't define a name such as *commission rate* because of the space. I'll frequently use an underscore (_) instead of a space. Another example is that you can't define the name *X123* because it conflicts with the built-in cell reference. For a more comprehensive discussion on name limitations and syntax rules, please refer to the Excel help system.

EXAMPLES

Let's work through some examples to get the hang of using Named References.

PRACTICE

If you'd like to play along with the next several examples, please refer to Named References.xlsx.

VIDEO

To watch me complete the exercises, please visit the Excel University video library at www.clickconsulting.com/books.

NAME A CELL QUICKLY

Our first example will demonstrate a quick way to name a cell.

PRACTICE

To follow along, please refer to the Exercise 1 worksheet.

In this example, you'll name a cell that stores a commission rate assumption and then refer to the rate inside of a commission calculation formula. First, activate the Commission rate value cell, D9 in Figure 5 below, either by clicking on it with your mouse or by navigating there with your newly mastered keyboard shortcuts.

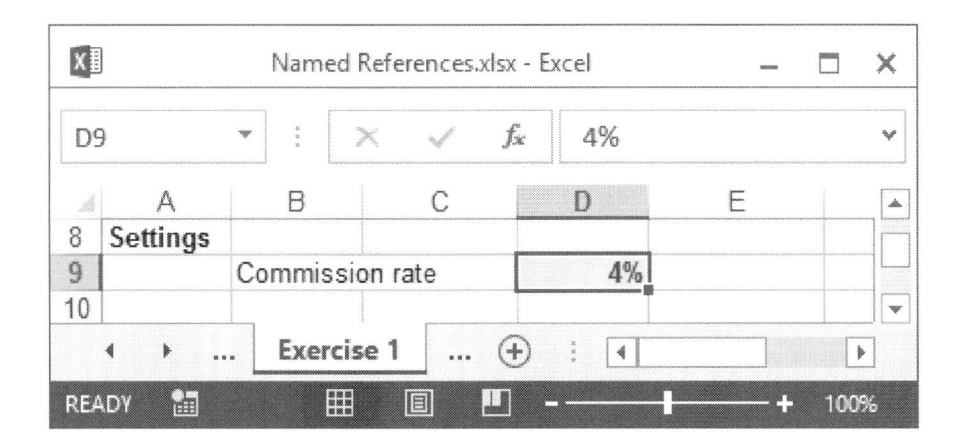

Figure 5

Next, type the desired name into the Name Box, which is the box immediately to the left of the formula bar. Since it is generally recommended to name cells with meaningful names, name the cell c_rate, to represent commission rate. After typing in the name, press the enter key on your keyboard. If the name you entered still appears in the Name Box, congratulations! You've successfully entered a Named Reference, as illustrated in Figure 6 below.

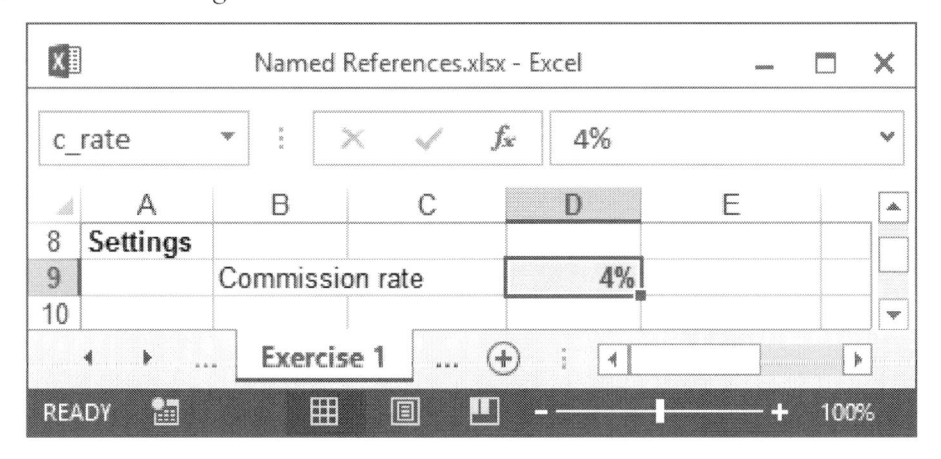

Figure 6

You should also notice that if you activate a cell with a name, the name will appear in the Name Box instead of the row/column reference. Now that you've successfully named the cell, you can use the name in a formula.

Since you need to compute the commission for each transaction, enter a commission formula (sales times rate) into the Commission column, as shown in Figure 7 below. To use the Named Reference (c_ rate) instead of the row/column reference (D9) in a formula, you have many options. To get the Named Reference into the formula as you write the formula, you could:

- Type the Named Reference either fully, or use the Tab key to auto-complete,
- Paste the Named Reference by pressing the F3 key on your keyboard, or
- Select the cell, and Excel will automatically insert the name rather than the row/column reference.

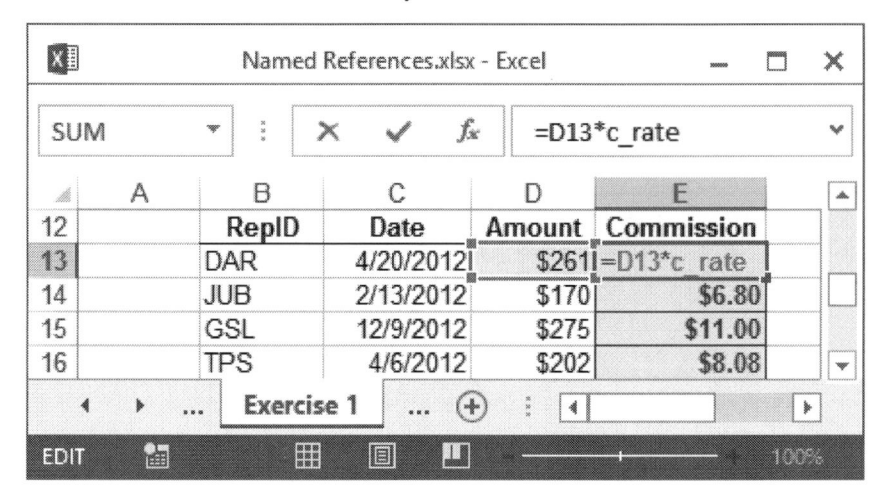

Figure 7

You'll notice that you didn't need to worry about converting the Named Reference into an absolute reference, which is what you would have had to do with a traditional row/column reference. This is because Named References are assumed to be absolute.

NAME A RANGE QUICKLY

Similar to naming a cell, you can name a range of cells. You can then use the name in any formulas that reference the range.

PRACTICE

To follow along, please refer to the Exercise 2 worksheet.

To get a feel for this, let's work through an example. First, you'll name a range of numbers and then use that name in a SUM function. Highlight the range E13:E25, enter the name amt_data in the Name Box, and press Enter, as illustrated in Figure 8 below.

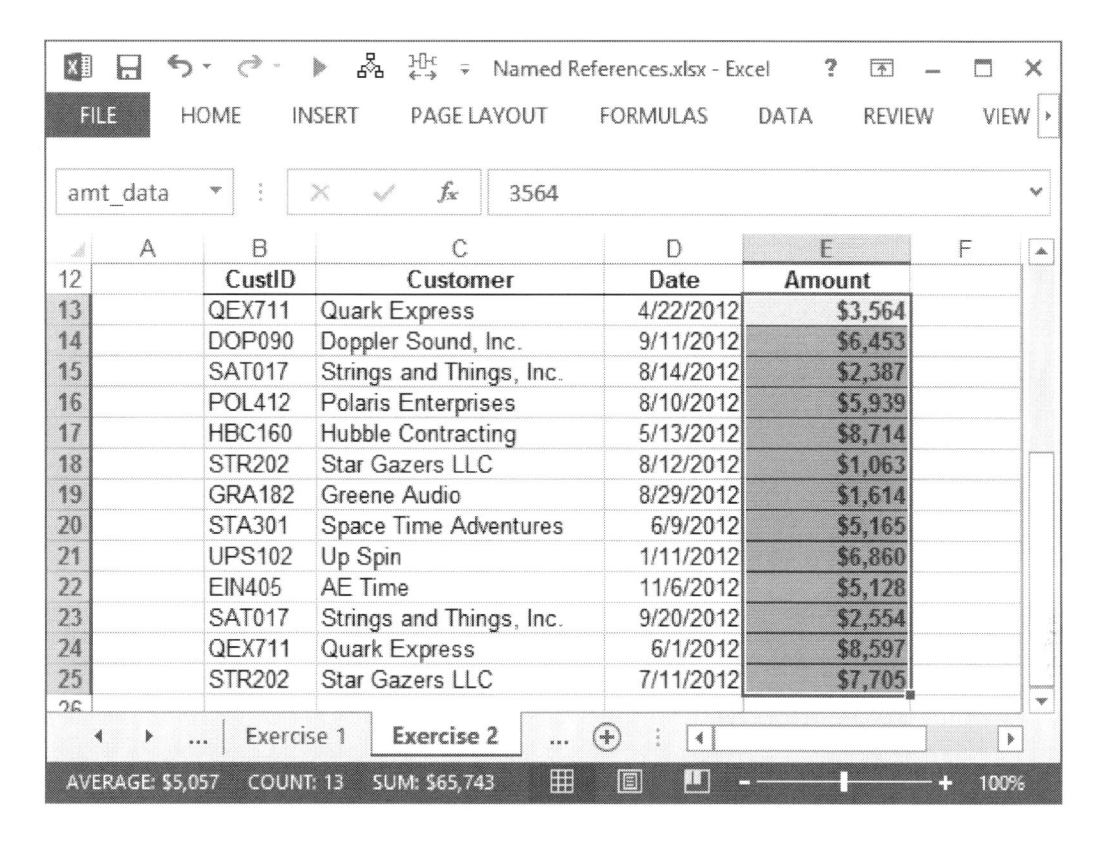

Figure 8

Now that you have successfully named the range, you can use it in formulas. To try it, write a SUM function in cell E9 that uses the name, as shown in Figure 9 below.

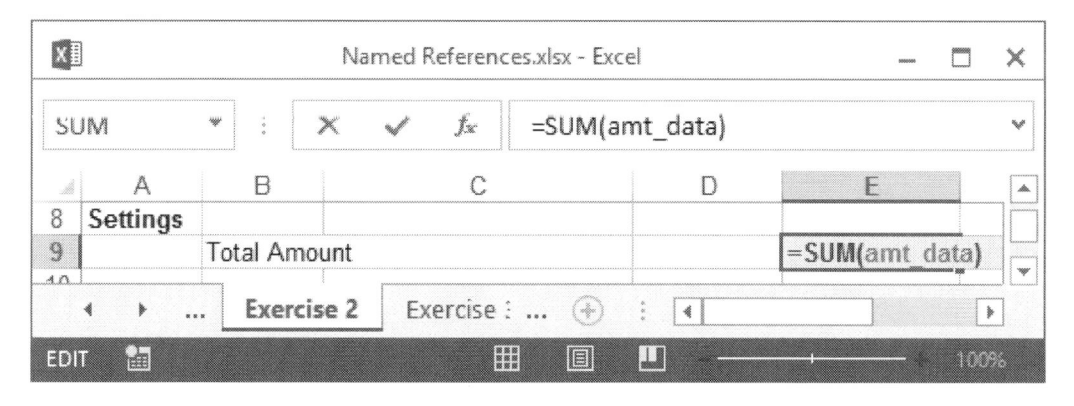

Figure 9

As you can see, using a name in a function makes the formula easier to understand and write, and it also eliminates the need to insert dollar signs to lock down the absolute cell reference. There are additional benefits to using Named References; let's explore now how they can help you navigate quickly through a workbook.

> **NOTE**
>
> You'll notice that Named References appear in the auto-complete list as you type them into formula cells. To insert a name (or other item) from the auto-complete list into the formula cell, use the Arrow keys (or mouse) to select the desired item from the drop-down list first, and then press Tab (or double-click) to auto-complete and insert it into the cell.

NAVIGATE

You can quickly navigate to a Named Reference. There are several ways to do this. One fast way is to select the Named Reference from the Name Box pull down.

> **PRACTICE**
>
> Follow along by using the Exercise 3 worksheet.

Try it now. Use the Name Box pull down and jump to one of the Named Referenced you previously set up in the workbook for example, amt_data, as shown in Figure 10 below.

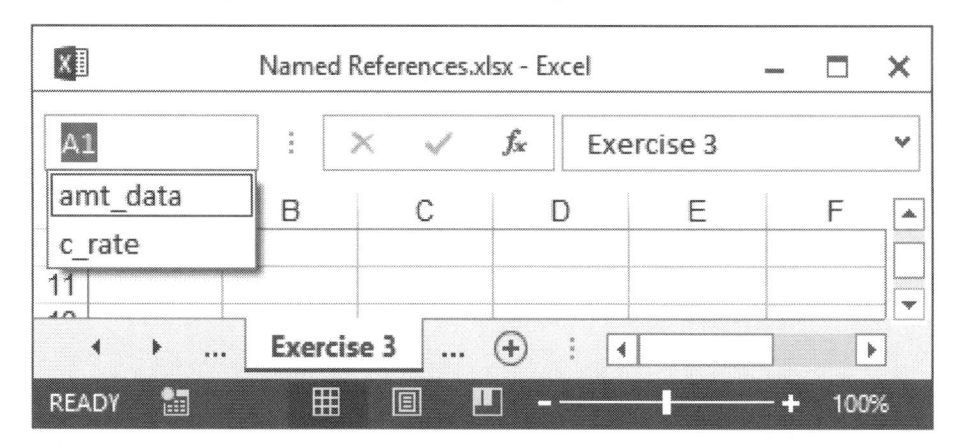

Figure 10

Another way to quickly jump to a Named Reference is by using the Go To feature. You can navigate to this feature as follows:

- RibbonUI: Home > Find & Select > Go To
- MenuUI: Edit > Go To

Activating the Go To feature calls up the Go To dialog box, as shown in Figure 11 below.

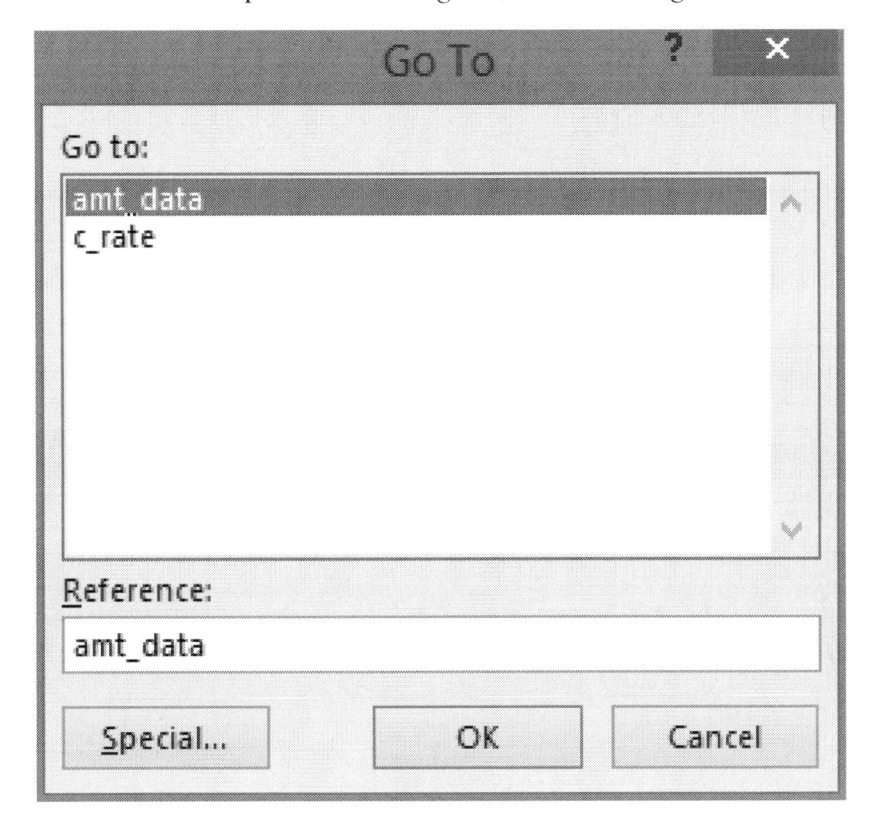

Figure 11

Select the Named Reference and click OK to be taken directly to it.

KB

Alternatively, you can use the F5 key on your keyboard as a shortcut to open the Go To dialog box.

XREF

Additional details about the Go To dialog are discussed in a subsequent book.

NAME MANAGER

Using the Name Box to define a Named Reference as described above is a shortcut. Use the Name Manager to manage names. With the Name Manager, you can edit an existing name, delete a name, set up a new name, or define advanced attributes like scope.

You can open the Name Manager as follows:

- RibbonUI: Formulas > Name Manager
- MenuUI: Insert > Name > Define

The Name Manager is shown in Figure 12 below.

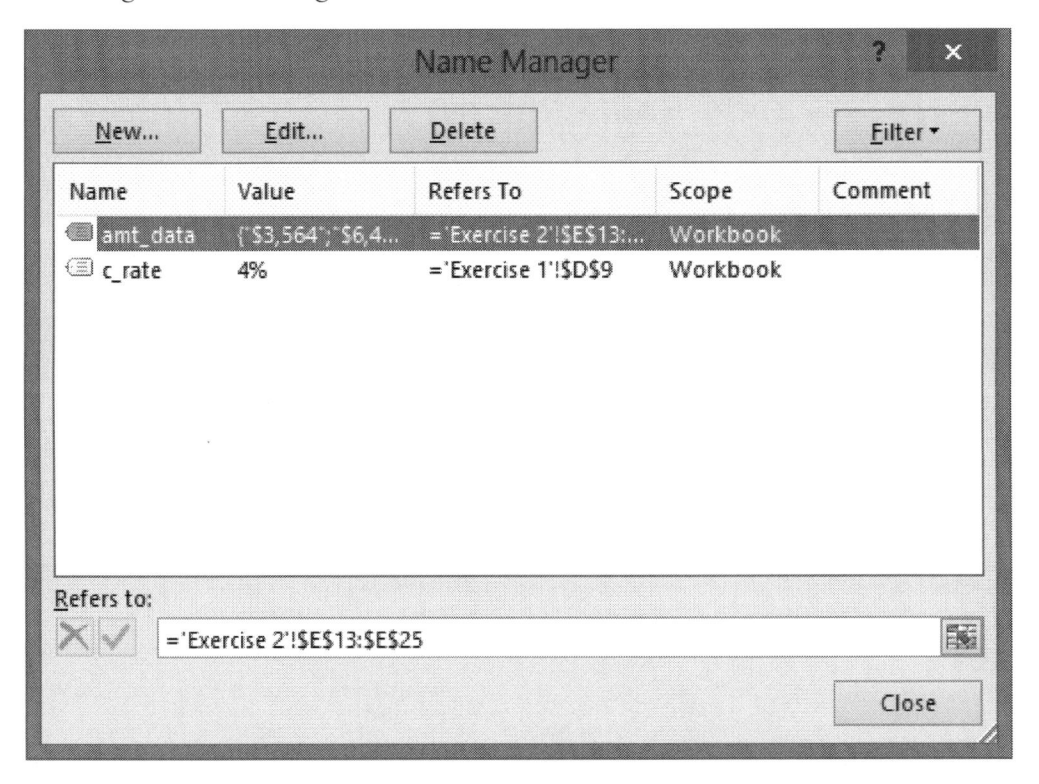

Figure 12

Within the Name Manager, you can add, edit, and delete names.

XREF

Named Reference Scope is discussed in a subsequent book.

PRACTICE

Please follow along with the Exercise 4 worksheet.

NOTE

You may notice that if you try to use your Arrow keys in the Refers To field in Figure 12, you'll actually be navigating the worksheet instead of navigating the dialog field. This is frustrating, since it will insert unwanted cell references into the field. Thus, press the F2 key to enter edit mode and your Arrow keys will work as expected.

New Name

To use the Name Manager to define a new name, simply click the New button to open the New Name dialog box. Here you'll be able to define the Name, the Scope (to be discussed in a later book), provide a useful Comment, and identify what the new name Refers to.

Try it now. The easiest way to start the process is by selecting the cell that you'd like to name. In this case, you want to name cell E10 on the practice worksheet. Next, open the Name Manager and create a new name st_rate that refers to the Sales Tax Rate value in cell E10, as shown in Figure 13 below.

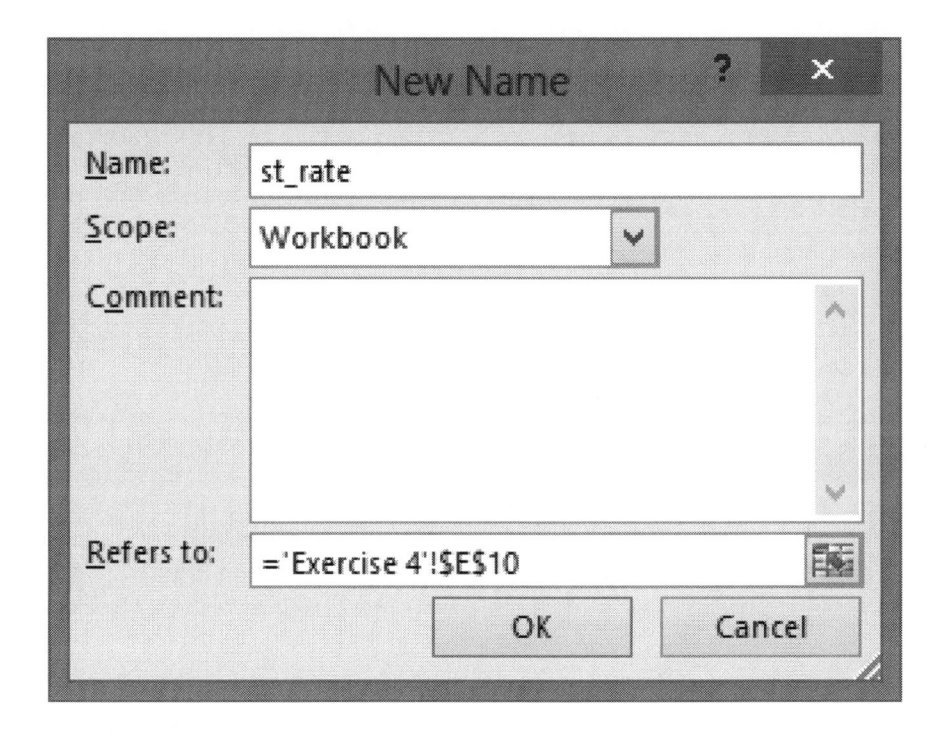

Figure 13

You'll notice that the Refers To field is already populated, since you opened the Name Manager after first selecting the cell. If the reference in the Refers To field is not correct, feel free to correct it by typing the right reference or by using your mouse or keyboard to select it on the worksheet.

> **NOTE**
>
> When defining Named References manually, be sure to use absolute cell references (unless you are performing some advanced task). Absolute references are set up by default when using the Name Box.

Change a Name

You can also use the Name Manager to edit either the name or the reference. Simply select the name you'd like to edit from the Name Manager and then click the Edit button. You'll be taken to the Edit Name dialog box, where you can simply change the values as desired.

Delete a Name

You can use the Name Manager to delete a Named Reference. Simply select the name you'd like to delete and then click the Delete button.

CHAPTER CONCLUSION

As you work through this course, you'll have plenty of opportunity to set up and use Named References.

When I create workbooks, I use Named References to name input cells used throughout a workbook, as well as ranges that are used in formulas on other worksheets. Generally, names are more important when the workbook will be in place for a while, such as for a recurring process.

Named references have certainly helped me create formulas that are easier to write, read, and maintain, and I hope they will help you too.

Chapter 8: Tables

The Tables feature was introduced in Excel 2007. Easily one of my favorite features, I use Tables all the time. I'm sure that as soon as you discover how effective Tables are, you'll use them all the time too.

SET UP

Probably one of the biggest pitfalls for Excel users is that Excel's range references don't automatically expand when a user enters additional data under the range. This pitfall results in worksheets that are error prone and inefficient. As a user enters new data under the range, the formulas that reference the range improperly exclude the new data, resulting in an error. To correct the error, the user needs to manually update or rewrite the formulas, which is inefficient. Let's look more closely at this issue. Suppose a worksheet has a SUM function that refers to the range A1:A10. (Actually, this example could include anything that refers to a range, such as a formula, function argument, chart, PivotTable, or any other worksheet object.) When a user enters data directly under the range, say in cell A11, the SUM function does not automatically update itself to include the new data. The new data in A11 is excluded because the SUM function was originally written to reference the range A1:A10. As you know, formulas don't automatically update their range references when new data is entered into cells outside of the original range. This is a pitfall, an error just waiting to happen.

> **NOTE**
>
> Formula range references do automatically update if a new row is inserted in the middle of the range, and that is wonderful. However, when new data is typed outside of the

range, the reference does not automatically update. This is the issue we are about to solve with Tables.

Even using Named References doesn't solve the problem, because any data entered immediately under the Named Reference will not automatically be included in the Named Reference.

This issue has plagued Excel users for a long time—a very long time.

Fortunately for us, Microsoft decided to address and resolve this issue in a very effective way with the Tables feature. Tables have many special properties that we need to investigate fully. So, without further ado, let's dig in.

HOW TO

A Table is essentially any range of data that has been defined as a Table. It is easy to convert a normal range of data into a Table by using the following command:

- RibbonUI: Insert > Table
- MenuUI: Feature unavailable

The Create Table dialog box appears as shown in Figure 14 below.

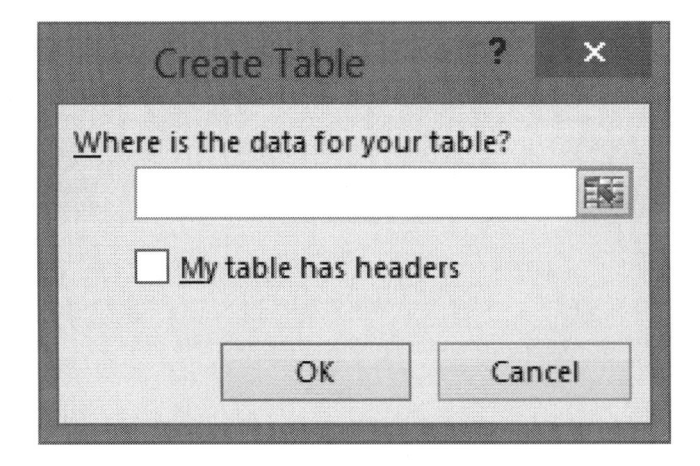

Figure 14

It is most efficient to select the data range, or a single cell within the data range, before launching the Create Table dialog, since the range reference will automatically be defined. If the first row of your data range has headers (labels), be sure to check the My Table Has Headers checkbox. Click OK to convert the normal data range into a Table.

KB

You can insert Tables with your keyboard: Ctrl+T or Alt+N, T.

Now that the normal range of data has been converted into a Table, it contains many special properties, including:

- Table Name
- Auto-Expansion
- Structured References
- Automatic Fill-Down
- Automatic Totals
- Column Label Replacement

EXAMPLES

Tables have several special properties. Let's work through each of these special properties using hands-on exercises, and we'll start with Table Name.

PRACTICE

To follow along with the upcoming examples, please refer to Tables.xlsx.

VIDEO

To watch me complete the exercises, please visit the Excel University video library at www.clickconsulting.com/books.

TABLE NAME

Each Table has a name that can be used in formulas, function arguments, and other places. A Table name is conceptually similar to the custom Named References we discussed previously. You can refer to the data in a Table by name, rather than with traditional A1 style references. Excel automatically assigns every Table a default name, such as Table1, Table2, and so on. (You can change the Table's default name, which we will cover shortly.)

PRACTICE

Follow along using with the Exercise 1 worksheet.

XREF

Named References are discussed in Chapter 7.

To convert a normal data range to a Table, first activate any cell within the region or select the entire region. Next, select the following Ribbon command:

- Insert > Table

Try it now; I'll wait. Go ahead and convert the range of data on the worksheet to a Table.

Once the range has been converted to a Table, you'll notice a couple of things. First you'll notice that Excel has applied some pretty formatting to the region. Next you'll see that there are drop down buttons on each column header. You'll also notice that a new Ribbon tab called Table Tools has appeared. The Table Tools Ribbon tab includes many buttons and controls that help you specify settings.

A Table's default name can be changed at any time. It is a good idea to get in the habit of changing the default name to a name that describes the data. Descriptive names help you stay organized: for example, tbl_coa for chart of accounts data, tbl_vendors for a vendor list, or tbl_employees for an employee list. To change the name, simply activate the Table by clicking any cell within and then edit the following Ribbon field:

- Tables Tools > Design > Table Name

Try it now. Change the name of the Table you created to tbl_data as shown in Figure 15 below.

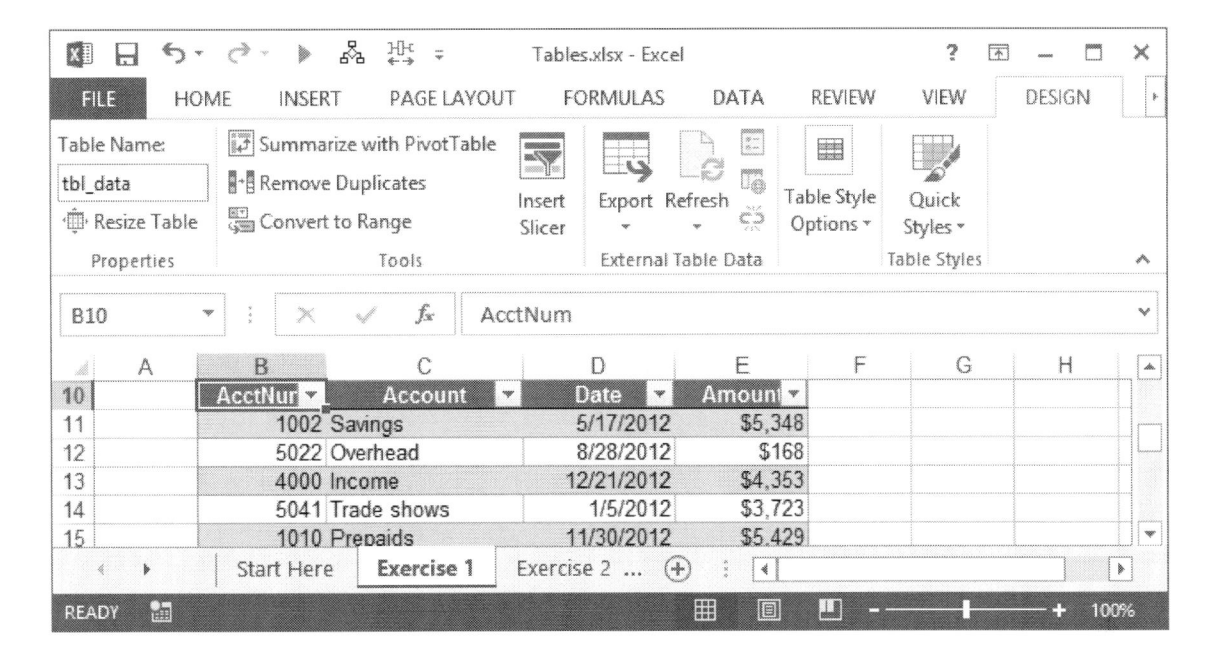

Figure 15

So far, we have converted a normal data region into a Table and have changed the default Table name to a more descriptive name. Now that we have a Table in a worksheet, let's explore some of the benefits.

AUTO-EXPANSION

One of the key properties of Tables is that they auto-expand to include new data. Think about that for a moment. Tables automatically expand to include new data a user types into cells immediately beneath (or to the right of) the Table.

This auto-expansion property helps us build workbooks that are more efficient and more accurate. If the benefit of this isn't immediately clear, I'll try to illustrate this with an example.

PRACTICE

Follow along with the Exercise 2 worksheet.

Chapter 8: Tables   69

First, convert the data region to a Table, and name it tbl_sales so that it has a descriptive name. Next, write a SUM function and use the Table name in the SUM function argument (rather than traditional row/column references) as follows:

```
=SUM(tbl_sales)
```

Where:

- **tbl_sales** is the range to sum

Now, here is the step that this has all been leading up to; type a value in the cell immediately under the Table. Bam! In the wise words of George Costanza, "Did you see what just happened here?" When you entered a value immediately under the Table, the Table automatically expanded itself to include the new data. Since you used the Table's name in the SUM function, the SUM function automatically included the new data. Wow!

As you can imagine, Tables represent a powerful approach to managing data regions, and they prevent errors and improve productivity. How do they prevent errors and improve productivity? Consider the previous exercise workbook. Without the use of a Table, the new data would have been excluded from the sum (an error). To correct the error, you would have had to manually edit the formula (inefficient). Thus, it is a good idea to convert ordinary data regions into Tables.

> **NOTE**
>
> Another approach to automatically include new data in formulas is to use column only references: for example, SUM(E:E) rather than SUM(E11:E17). Column-only references are appropriate in some situations, and when they are, I'll absolutely use them. However, Tables provide many benefits and thus they are my preferred approach in most situations.

> **NOTE**
>
> Tables will automatically expand when the new data is entered immediately under the Table, which means no blank rows. If there is a blank row, the Table will not auto-expand. Additionally, a copy/paste of data will also expand the Table provided the paste isn't an entire row, for example Row 10.

> **NOTE**
>
> Besides using Table names in formulas and function arguments, you can use them as source data for objects such as PivotTables.

Besides auto-expansion, Tables have other special properties: for example, Structured References.

STRUCTURED REFERENCES

Think of Structured References as names that refer to certain areas within a Table, for example, a specific column. Structured reference names begin with the Table name, followed by the specific Table area surrounded by square brackets []. For example, the name Table1[Amount] refers to the Amount column of a Table named Table1.

In addition to specific columns, you can refer to other areas within the Table, for example the header row, the data region, or the total row. I find the most useful references are the column references and the header row. Here are many of the available references:

- TableName[ColumnName] – refers to the specific column of data excluding the header row
- TableName[#All] – refers to all columns, including data, headers and total row, if any
- TableName[#Data] – refers to all columns, data only (excludes header and total rows)
- TableName[#Headers] – refers to top header row only
- TableName[#Totals] – refers to total row only
- TableName[@] – refers to the current row (the same row that this reference is in)

To insert a structured reference into a formula, you can either select the region with your mouse or keyboard, or type it in. To type it in, begin by entering the table name and then the open square bracket. A drop down list will appear with the various reference choices. To select the one you want either double click it with your mouse, or use the down Arrow on your keyboard and the Tab key to auto-complete.

🔘 PRACTICE

To follow along, refer to the Exercise 3 worksheet.

First, convert the Trial Balance data in the worksheet to a Table named tbl_tb. Next, write a SUM function to sum the Debit column, as shown below:

```
=SUM(tbl_tb[Debit])
```

Where:

- **tbl_tb[Debit]** is the range to sum, the Debit column of the tbl_tb table.

Write another SUM function to sum the Credit column.

As you can see, structured references enable the inclusion of specific columns in functions and formulas and help unlock the power of Tables.

AUTOMATIC FILL-DOWN

Another special property of Tables is automatic formula fill-down. If a Table has a calculation column, and the same formula is used for all rows in the column, Excel will automatically fill the formula down as new data rows are added to the Table. As you can imagine, this makes the workbook easier to maintain, since a human no longer needs to babysit the formula to ensure it is filled down through all new rows.

🔘 PRACTICE

Try it now! Follow along with the Exercise 4 worksheet.

Start this exercise by converting the data region to a Table, using tbl_taxdata for the Table name. Next, insert a custom Named Reference t_rate for the Tax Rate value. Finally, write a formula in the first cell in the Sales Tax column to compute sales tax. You'll notice how Excel took the liberty of filling your formula down through all rows of the Table. Even as you add new data, Excel will babysit this field and ensure that it is filled down through all rows of the Table. That is yet another efficiency boost we gain by using Tables.

DEPENDS ON

The completion of this exercise depends on knowledge of Named References, discussed in Chapter 7.

AUTOMATIC TOTALS

You can automatically insert a total row at the end of a Table, by selecting the following Ribbon command:

- Table Tools > Design > Total Row

NOTE

The Table Tools Ribbon tab only appears when a Table is active (that is, when you've selected a cell or range in the Table).

Excel will try to guess which column requires a total and the type of total. However, if Excel guesses incorrectly, it is easy to make changes. Changing the math is easy: simply use the pull down control that is in the total cell, pictured in Figure 16.

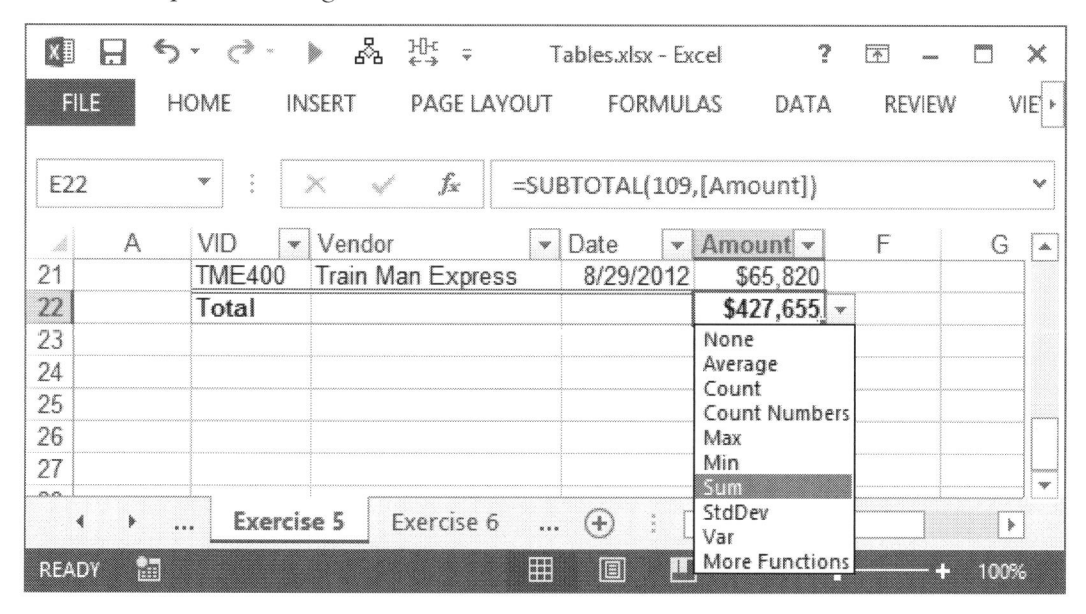

Figure 16

In addition, you can add totals to other columns simply by using the pull down for any column in the total row.

Chapter 8: Tables

PRACTICE

Follow along with the Exercise 5 worksheet.

XREF

You may notice that the function Excel uses to compute a total is the SUBTOTAL function. This amazing function is discussed in Chapter 11.

Give it a try. Convert the vendor purchases data region to a Table named tbl_vendor_purchases and then add a Total Row by checking the Total Row checkbox from the Table Tools ribbon.

COLUMN LABEL REPLACEMENT

One subtle but convenient aspect of using Tables is that as you scroll down a worksheet, the Table column headers will replace the standard Excel column labels (A, B, C, etc), if the Table is active (if a cell or range within the Table is selected).

PRACTICE

Follow along with the Exercise 6 worksheet.

If you want to see this in action, convert the data region to a Table named tbl_transactions and then be sure to activate the Table by selecting any portion of it. The standard Excel column labels will appear as normal, as shown in Figure 17 below.

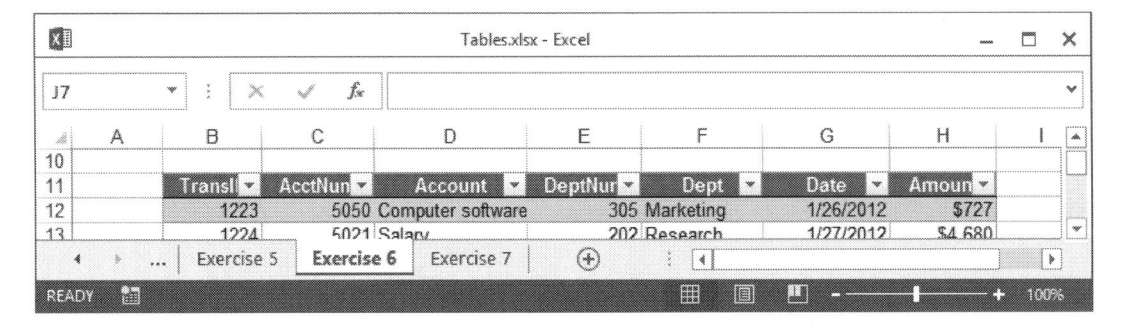

Figure 17

However, as you scroll down the worksheet while the Table remains active, you'll notice that Excel replaces the standard column labels (A, B, C …) with the Table's column headers, as shown in Figure 18 below.

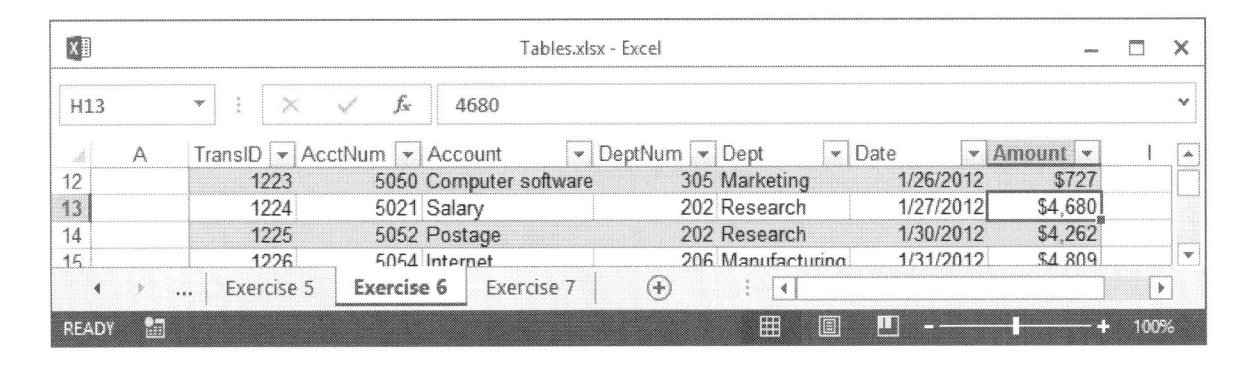

Figure 18

This is useful when working within large Tables, as it eliminates the traditional need to freeze rows. Beginning with Excel 2010, in addition to showing the column header, Excel also includes a drop down control for easy sorting and filtering.

OTHER RIBBON SETTINGS

Thus far, I've highlighted the Table features I believe to be the most useful. However, in addition to the specific Table features discussed above, you can play with several other settings. I'll quickly discuss the additional features, but for a more comprehensive explanation please refer to the Excel built-in help system.

PRACTICE

To follow along, please refer to the Exercise 7 worksheet.

Create a Table from the Check data region. While the Table is active, you have access to the Table Tools Design ribbon tab. Please feel free to play with the buttons described below:

- Resize Table – click this button to change the source region of the Table

- Summarize with PivotTable – a shortcut for generating a PivotTable using the Table as the source

- Remove Duplicates – a shortcut for removing duplicate transactions within the Table

- Convert to Range – remove the Table

- External Table Data buttons – various buttons to export Table data to other places

- Table Style Option checkboxes – turn on or off various items, including the Total Row, Header Row, and various style settings
- Table Styles – a palette of various style selections and color choices. You can mask the fact that a data region is a Table by changing the style to "None"

CHAPTER CONCLUSION

And that, my friend, concludes our discussion of Tables. It is my hope that you find as much benefit from them as I have, and don't worry, we'll be playing with them more during our time together.

ADDITIONAL RESOURCES

For additional information, please refer to my article **"Excel Rules,"** published in the May 2010 *California CPA Magazine's Technology & Business Resource Guide*, available online at clickconsulting.com or calcpa.org.

This piece walks through Tables and SUMIFS and provides additional information, examples, and details of these two features.

It covers Tables and the special properties, as well as some practical examples for SUMIFS, such as automating reports from a QuickBooks extract.

Chapter 9: Data Validation

Data Validation is one of my favorite features, and one that I use in many of my workbooks. It is a fundamental feature to know and understand, and we'll revisit it often throughout our time together.

SET UP

Technically, the Data Validation (DV) feature is designed to control what a user can type in to a cell. But in practice it is much more powerful than that. We'll begin by illustrating this feature with some simple examples, but throughout the series, we'll expand our use of the DV feature. I'm so excited that I hardly know where to begin.

Data Validation allows you to control what a user can type in to a cell. For example, if you have a cell that requires an entry of a date between January 1 and January 31, you can turn on Data Validation for that cell, and Excel will only allow the user to enter a valid date. You define what is valid by setting up the validation rule. Following are a few rules to give you an idea of how DV works:

- Allow an account number (whole number) between 1 and 1000
- Allow a decimal number between 1 and 5
- Allow a date between a range of dates
- Allow only a positive number (a number greater than zero)
- Allow only a value from a list of choices

The built-in validation rules are fairly comprehensive, but when they are insufficient for your needs, you can set up custom rules. Now that you have an idea of what DV does, let's discuss when to use it.

If I am both the workbook administrator and the workbook user, I may or may not take time to set up Data Validation. If however, someone else is the workbook user who maintains the data in the workbook on an ongoing basis, you bet I'll take time to set up Data Validation. You see, Data Validation helps to prevent errors from happening. If you are familiar with internal controls, Data Validation is more like a preventive control than a detective control.

Data Validation is the feature I use to provide a list of choices with an in-cell drop down. I'll almost always set up an in-cell drop down when I build a formula that is designed to evaluate only certain values. If a user enters a value into a cell that my formula is not designed to handle, unexpected results will occur, but a DV rule avoids this conflict. For example, let's say that I have a formula that performs a lookup of a month. The formula expects the user to enter the month using a three-letter abbreviation, such as Jan, Feb, or Mar. If the user enters the month using a different format, perhaps a two-letter abbreviation, a numeric abbreviation, or the month name spelled out, the formula will break. That is, the formula will return either an error or a bogus result. To prevent this issue, I'll set up an in-cell drop down to limit the user's entry to the values that my formula is designed to handle.

In addition, Data Validation helps ensure that data is entered into a worksheet consistently, enabling the use of some of Excel's advanced features. For example, let's say there is a data input range on a worksheet and one of the columns is Month. Various users enter data into the worksheet over time. Sometimes, they type Jan, 1, or January to indicate January. Now, you have three or more representations of the same underlying value, January. This means that you are prevented from using some of Excel's advanced features. You see, you can't use a PivotTable to summarize the data because to a PivotTable, Jan, 1, and January are three different months. Even to worksheet functions such as SUMIFS and to features such as Auto Filter, the values represent three different months. Thus, ensuring data consistency is important: for example, that January is always entered the same way, or that rep and department names are always entered the same way. You can probably imagine dozens of other examples. Data Validation helps ensure data consistency. Additionally, we can use a deadly combination of Data Validation and the CHOOSE function to enable some spectacular functionality within a workbook. Since the technique is somewhat advanced, we will cover the details in a future book. But here is an example of how it works: Consider a workbook designed to help a manager budget her upcoming SG&A expenses. You could allow her to select a budget method for each account from a DV in-cell drop down. Then, your super cool formula would perform different math equations depending on her choice.

For example, if she selects Spread PY from the drop down, then the formula will return prior year actuals divided by 12 (months). If she selects Match PY from the drop down, then the formula will return prior year actual values for each month. If she selects Headcount from the drop down, then the formula will apply prior year actual divided by prior year headcount to her upcoming budgeted headcount. You see, the formula performs different math depending on what she selected from the DV drop down. Cool? Yes.

Let's do one more example. We could set up a workbook that allows the user to select the depreciation method from a drop down. Depending on the depreciation method chosen, the formulas compute straight line, declining balance, double-declining balance, or sum-of-the-years digits accordingly. Those are two examples of the power of using Data Validation along with the CHOOSE function. As you can tell, this technique allows us to set up some very useful workbooks.

XREF

The CHOOSE function is covered in a subsequent book.

NOTE

The Data Validation feature is effective when a user types or enters a value into a cell. Unfortunately, it does not prevent a user from copy/pasting an invalid value into the cell. This is because a typical Paste command replaces everything in the destination cell, including Data Validation settings. That is, when the user pastes in the value from the source cell, they also paste in the Data Validation settings of the source cell. If the source cell has no validation settings, then the paste essentially wipes out the Data Validation settings of the destination cell. One workaround to this limitation is discussed in the VBA/macro section in a subsequent book. I never let this limitation prevent me from using DV.

OK, I hope my long-winded discussion above has been enough to get you pumped up and ready to explore Data Validation. If you haven't played with Data Validation yet, I'm glad to be able to introduce this feature to you, and in the wise words of Adrian Monk, "You'll thank me later." Now, let's get started!

HOW TO

To apply Data Validation to a cell (or range), begin by selecting the cell (or range). Next, activate the Data Validation dialog box by:

- RibbonUI: Data > Data Validation
- MenuUI: Data > Data Validation

KB

The keyboard shortcut I use to open the Data Validation dialog is Alt+D, L (data validation), which comes from the old Menu UI. Alternatively, you can use Alt+A, V, V, which comes from the Ribbon UI. Both commands work in the Ribbon UI.

You'll find that the Data Validation dialog box has three tabs, Settings, Input Message, and Error Alert, as shown in Figure 19 below.

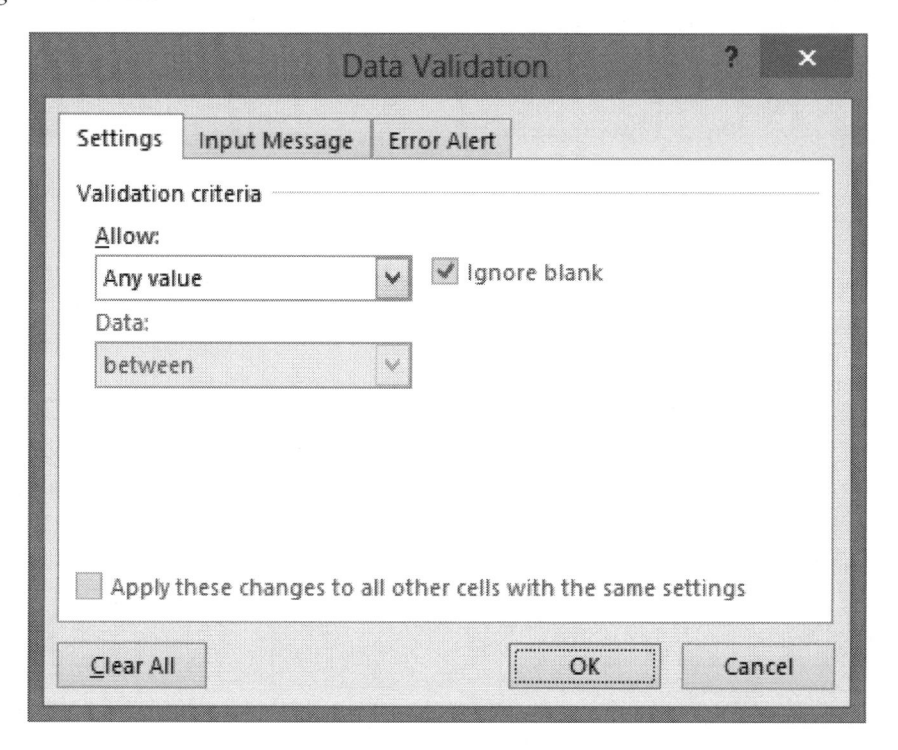

Figure 19

- The Settings tab is where you set the rule that defines a valid entry: for example, any whole number between 1 and 1000 or any date between 12/1/12 and 12/31/12.

- The Input Message tab is where you optionally define a message that will pop up when the cell is selected: for example, "Please enter a whole number between 1 and 1000."

- The Error Alert tab is where you optionally define a message that will pop up when the user enters invalid data, for example: "Error: Please enter a whole number between 1 and 1000."

All right, let's work through some of the details of this feature with a few practice exercises.

PRACTICE

The following practice exercises will demonstrate many aspects of Data Validation.

🔘 PRACTICE

To follow along, please refer to Data Validation.xlsx.

▶ VIDEO

To watch me complete the exercises, please visit the Excel University video library at www.clickconsulting.com/books.

DECIMAL

We'll start with a simple warm-up exercise. Let's say you have a handful of Excel forms that employees need to fill out from time to time. The forms are used to process items such as expense reimbursements, travel requests, PTO requests, and purchase requests. Employees complete the forms in Excel by entering values into the various input cells. Currently, employees can enter any value in any of the input cells in the various forms. When an employee submits the form, the manager reviews the input fields to ensure that they conform to company policies, such as meals and entertainment expenses being capped at $75 per day and valid account and department numbers being used. Forms submitted with invalid data create inefficiency, since the manager must send the form back to the employee and then perform an additional review. Because you'd like to improve efficiency by reducing the number of forms submitted with invalid data, you decide to implement the Data Validation feature.

🔘 PRACTICE

To follow along, please refer to the Exercise 1 worksheet.

The company policy for meal reimbursement is a max of $75 per day. Currently, the employee can enter any value into the Excel form, even if it does not comply with the policy.

Consider the simplified travel expense form in Figure 20 below.

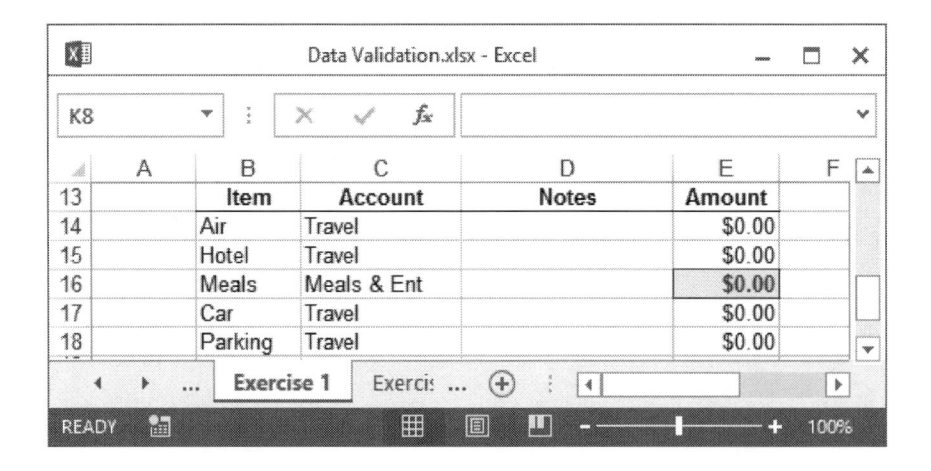

Figure 20

Your objective is to restrict the Meals Amount (cell E16) to any decimal between $0 and $75. Any entries outside of this range should be considered invalid.

To activate Date Validation, select cell E16 and then open the Data Validation dialog box. From the Settings tab allow a decimal between 0 and 75, as shown in Figure 21 below.

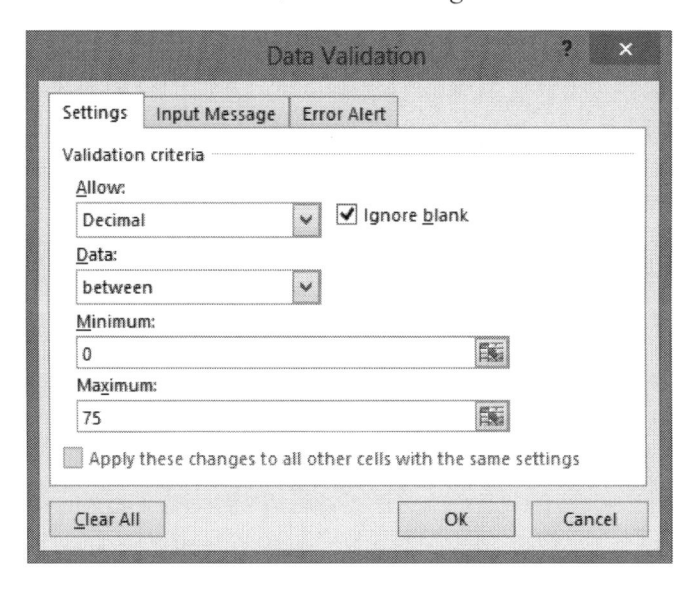

Figure 21

Now, test it! Try to enter a good number, such as 50. Excel should allow you to enter 50 since it is valid, as defined. Try to enter a bad number, such as 100. Excel should display an error message. If not, please go back and double check the Data Validation settings for the cell.

As you can imagine, limiting entry to valid data will improve the efficiency of many processes, since the number of errors that need to be caught and corrected is reduced.

WHOLE NUMBER

Suppose that you have a form, and a cell in the form requires the employee to enter a department number. Currently your department numbers range from 100 to 999. You'd like to prevent the employee from entering a number outside of this range, so you set up Data Validation.

PRACTICE

To follow along, please refer to the Exercise 2 worksheet.

Since there are no department numbers with decimal values, you define the rule on the Settings tab to allow a whole number between 100 and 999.

In order to communicate the validation rule with the employee, you decide to define a custom input message. Within the Data Validation dialog box, use the Input Message tab to define the custom message "Please enter a valid department number between 100 and 999," as shown in Figure 22 below.

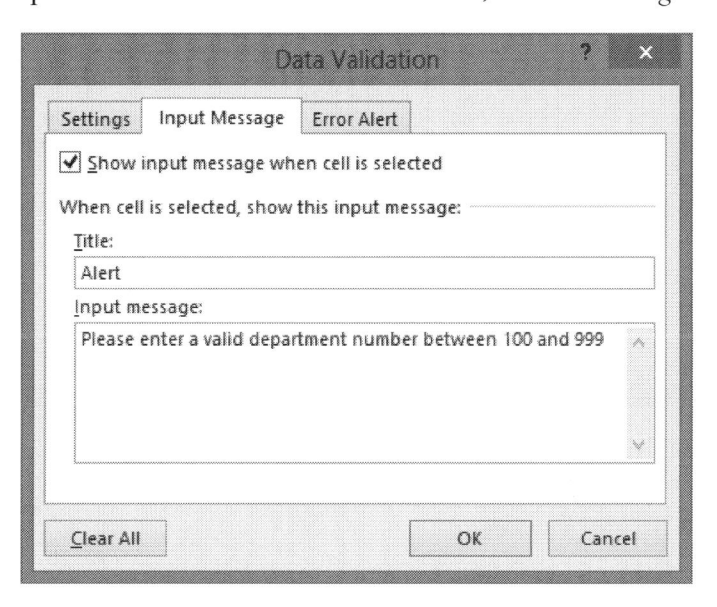

Figure 22

Now, try it out! Select the Department cell and ensure that the input message pops up as shown in Figure 23 below. Try to enter invalid data and verify that Excel displays an error message.

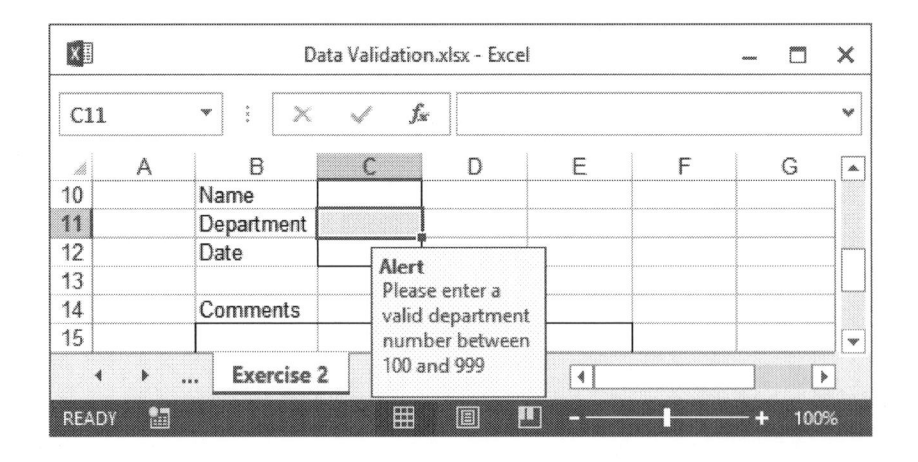

Figure 23

> **NOTE**
>
> The employee enters the department number into the input cell C11. If you'd like to display the department name in a different cell, say, D11, use a lookup function such as VLOOKUP. Lookup functions are discussed in a subsequent book.

Now, let's customize the error message that pops up when an employee enters invalid data. Go back into the Data Validation dialog box and set the Error Alert to read, "Please enter a valid dept number between 100 and 999," as shown in Figure 24 below.

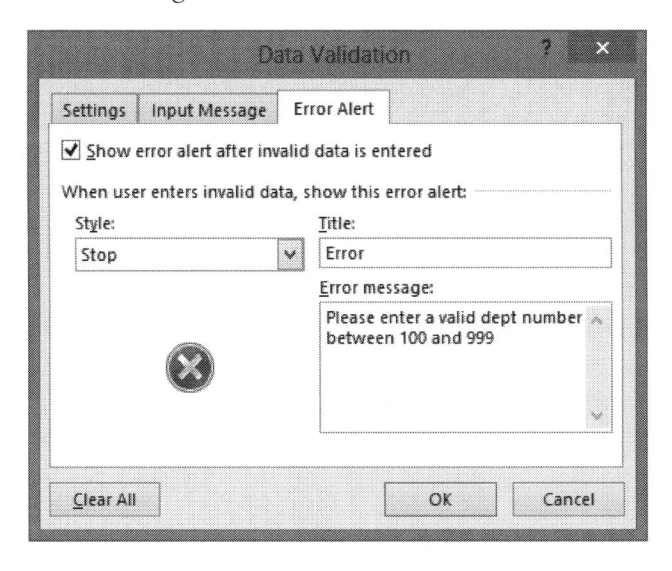

Figure 24

Please use the Error Alert Style, Stop, for this exercise. The other styles (Warning and Information) display different icons and allow the user to override the Data Validation setting. Generally you'll want to use Stop for your workbooks. Feel free to play with the other styles and check them out.

XREF

Additional Data Validation features, including alert styles, are discussed in detail in a subsequent book.

Now, enter some invalid data, and ensure that your customized Error alert pops up as shown in Figure 25 below.

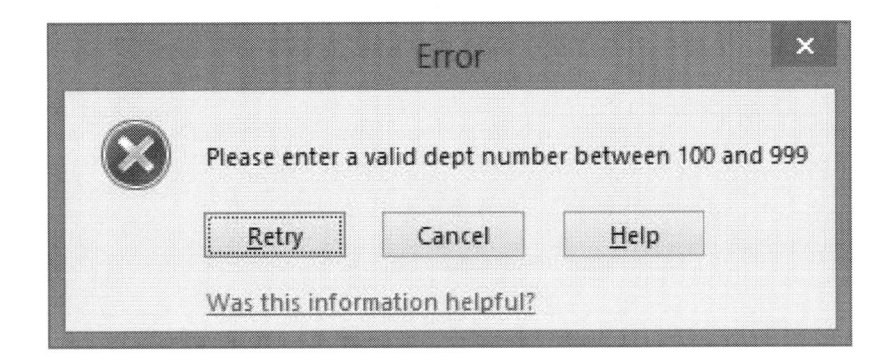

Figure 25

LIST ON SAME SHEET

Now that you are warmed up, let's get to the good stuff. For the most part, I primarily use the Data Validation feature to provide in-cell drop down lists. Probably 90% of the time that I use this feature, I use it to provide drop down lists. So the remaining exercises are designed to progressively walk through this use.

Do you recall the earlier exercise that asked you to limit the input cell to a valid department number between 100 and 999? In reality, not every whole number between 100 and 999 represents a valid department number. So, rather than simply limit the input to any whole number between 100 and 999, we need the ability to limit the input to a specific list of valid department numbers. That is, a list of choices. The Data Validation feature provides a convenient way to offer a list of choices in an in-cell drop down.

PRACTICE

To follow along, please refer to the Exercise 3 worksheet.

Setting up an in-cell drop down is easy. The key thing to remember is that you want to Allow a List. In the Settings tab of the DV dialog, select List for the Allow option. Next, identify the list of choices using the Source field. The Source field is flexible and allows you to specify the list a couple of different ways. For example, the Source field can be expressed as a comma-delimited list, such as "Mon, Tues, Wed, Thurs, Fri." Rather than define the source with a comma-delimited list, it is generally more convenient to refer to a range of cells.

In this exercise, use the department list found in cells B13:B23 for the Source field (i.e., the list of choices). The DV settings dialog should be similar to Figure 26 below.

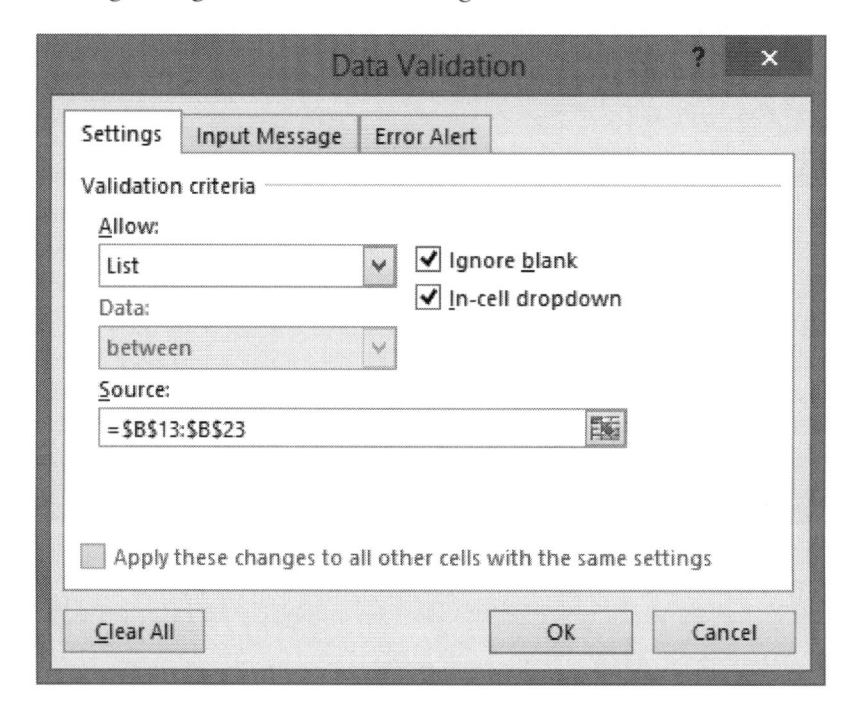

Figure 26

Once the DV settings are applied, the in-cell drop down control activates when a user selects the cell. Clicking the drop-down control reveals the list of choices, as shown in Figure 27 below.

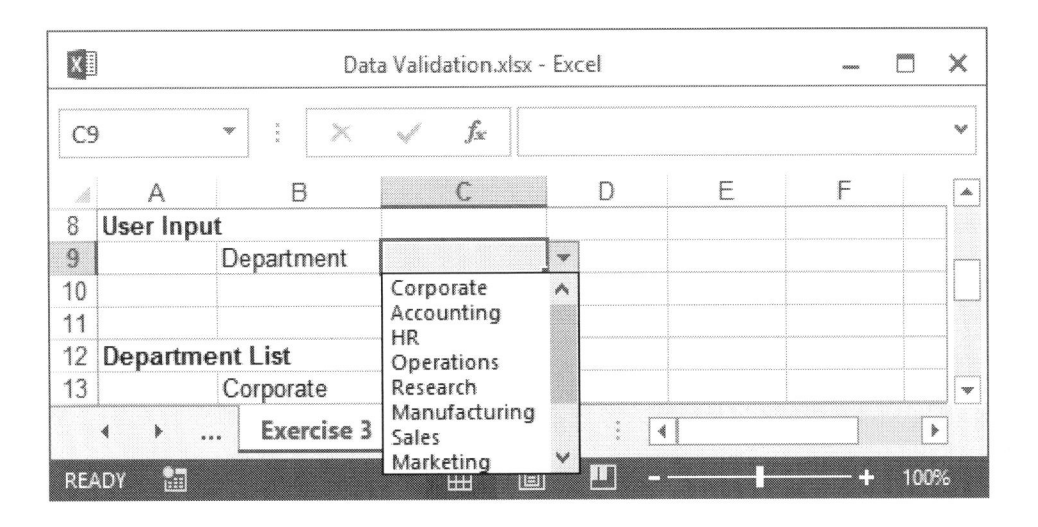

Figure 27

Now, the user can select a choice from the list using the nifty in-cell drop down.

> **NOTE**
>
> Please note that a user may enter a value into the cell either by interacting with the drop down control (i.e., clicking the drop down and selecting an item), or by typing a value. Data Validation evaluates the value, even if typed in, and prevents the cell from storing an invalid value (i.e., a value that isn't in the drop down list).

> **NOTE**
>
> Unfortunately, as of the time of this writing, Excel does not auto-complete the cell if a user begins to type in the first few characters of a valid choice. Perhaps Microsoft will add this feature in a future version; let's hope!

> **KB**
>
> When navigating in the worksheet, pull down the in-cell drop down with: Alt+Down Arrow. Repeatedly pressing the down Arrow key moves the cursor down the list. Use the Enter key to select the item.

LIST ON DIFFERENT SHEET

In this exercise, you'll set up an in-cell drop down for a data entry region and use a source range that is located on a different worksheet.

So far the examples have focused on validating a single entry cell. Sometimes however, a user needs to input multiple transactions. When a user enters a series of transactions, you need a way to ensure that the data is entered consistently. If the user does not enter the data consistently, the advanced features of Excel can't be used effectively.

For example, let's say that your user needs to enter a series of transactions, and one of the columns is the client name. After all of the transactions are entered, you plan to use some of Excel's advanced features to analyze the data, for example, PivotTables, AutoFilters, and charts. Your user must enter the client names consistently if these advanced features are to be used. For example, consider the client name "ABC Associates, Inc." You would have a mess if your user inconsistently entered the client name in the various transactions, using for example, "ABC Associates," "ABC Associates Inc," "ABC Associates, Inc.," and "ABC Assoc." To any of Excel's features and functions, those are different clients, not the same client. Thus, Excel would not be able to properly group and aggregate transactions based on client name. In the end, you'd have a big mess to clean up.

Rather than risk a big cleanup at the end, you decide to implement Data Validation and prevent those types of inconsistencies from occurring in the first place.

PRACTICE

To follow along, please refer to the Exercise 4 worksheet.

Highlight the data entry range for the Client column (C12:C16) and then open the Data Validation dialog box. You want to Allow a List. To identify the Source list of choices, simply highlight the range that contains the choices on the source worksheet (Exercise 4 List). Generally, it is best practice to keep lists like this on a different sheet, and I make a habit of centrally storing all lists for a workbook on a single worksheet.

NOTE

If you are following along with Excel 2007 or earlier, you won't be able to browse to a different sheet. This is only allowed beginning with Excel 2010. To use a cell range from a different sheet with older versions of Excel, you'll need to use Named References, as discussed below.

Apply the DV settings and then test it out. Navigate to the cells and ensure that you see the in-cell drop down list as shown in Figure 28 below.

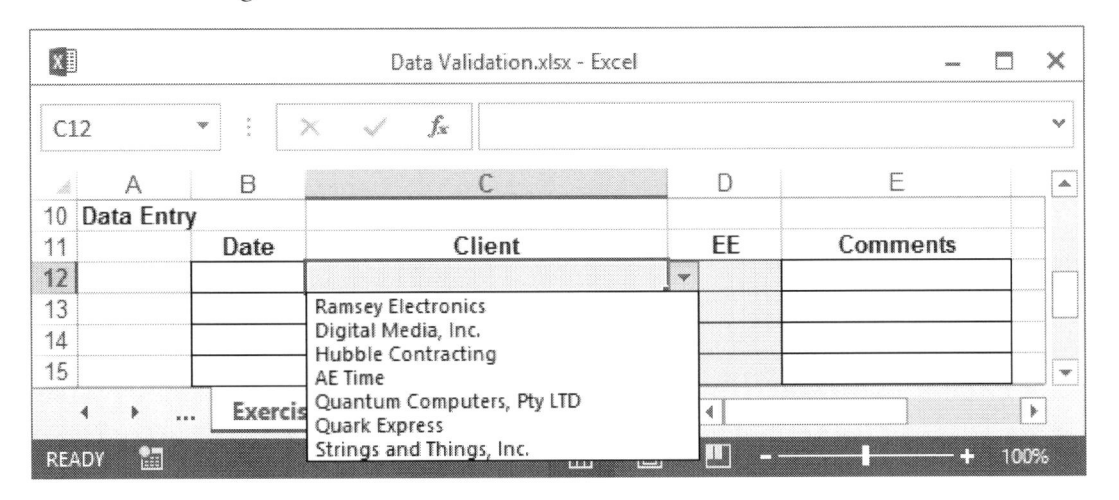

Figure 28

Using DV in this manner is a wonderful approach to reducing inconsistencies in your workbooks.

LIST WITH NAMED REFERENCE

In this exercise, you want to allow your user to enter a month into a cell. Your workbook has some powerful lookup functions that refer to the month. These smart worksheet functions are set up to handle months entered with three-letter abbreviations, such as Jan, Feb, or Mar. If the user enters the month in a different way, for example, the month name spelled out (January, February or March) or as a number (1, 2 or 3), then the formula will break. This means that the user may unintentionally break the workbook simply by using a different representation of the month. This would undoubtedly surprise and frustrate the user, so you want to address this issue.

In the above example, I used the idea that the user would break the workbook, but let's dig in to that a bit. To be clear, the user wouldn't break the workbook. Technically, the formulas were not written to evaluate all possible variations of month names. The formulas were written to evaluate the three-letter abbreviations.

So, rather than write more sophisticated formulas that would handle all variations of months, you decide simply to restrict what the user can enter. That sounds like a job for the Data Validation feature.

PRACTICE

To follow along, please refer to the Exercise 5 worksheet.

DEPENDS ON

This content depends on knowledge of the Named References feature, discussed in Chapter 7.

Begin by setting up a range that contains the month abbreviations that the formulas are designed to process. (If you are following along, this has been done already on the Exercise 5 List worksheet). This range of cells will be used as the source for choices listed in the in-cell drop down.

Next, assign the range a meaningful name (Named Reference), such as months. After you have set up the Named Reference, it is time to set up DV on the input cell. So, select the input cell and then open the Data Validation dialog box and assign a validation rule to Allow a List. The Source for the list is the Named Reference you just set up. The trick here is that you must precede the Named Reference with an equal sign, as shown in Figure 29 below.

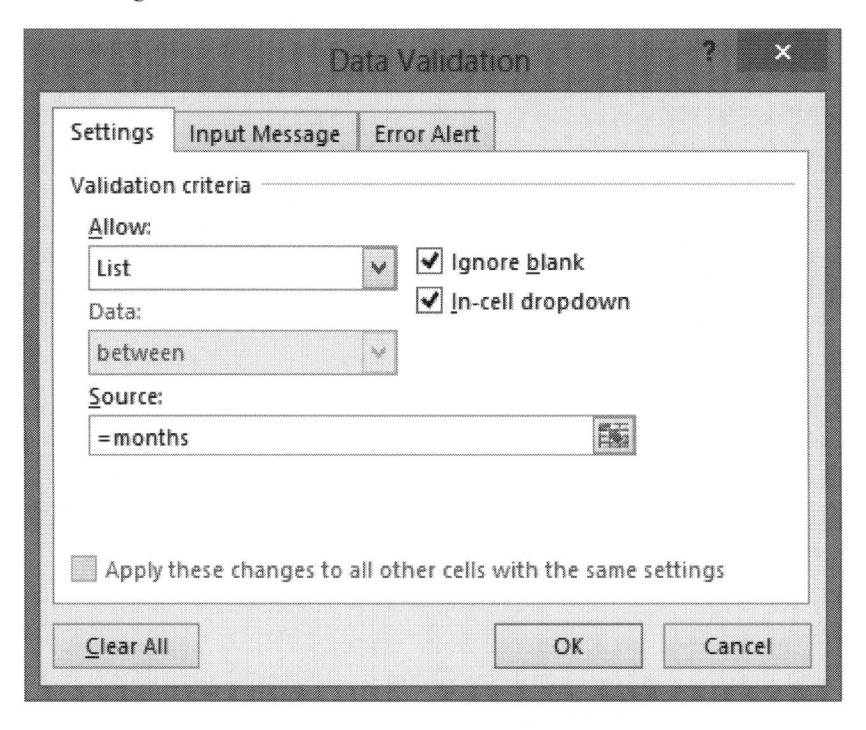

Figure 29

Now, test it. Select the input cell and ensure that the in-cell drop down contains the months as expected as shown in Figure 30 below.

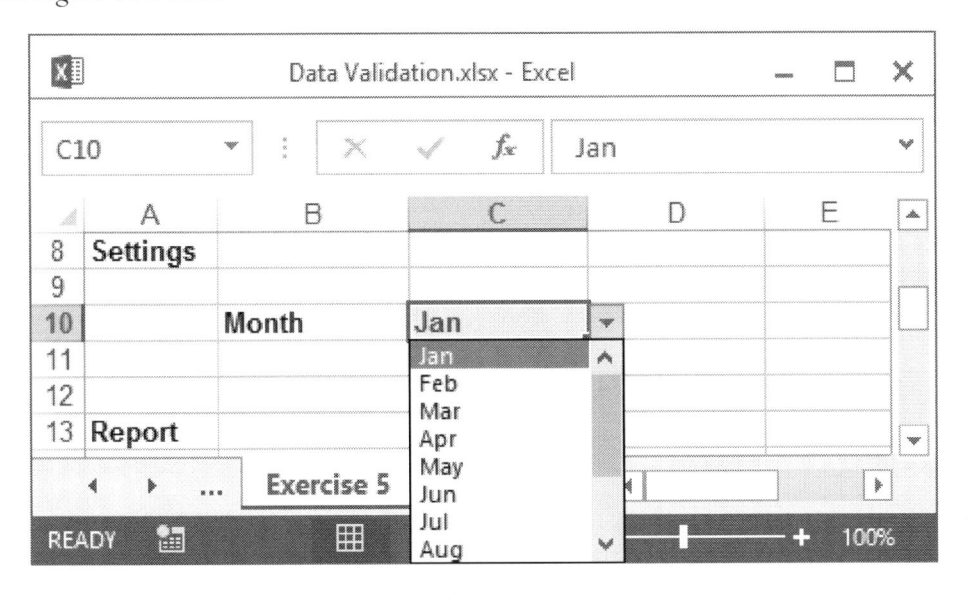

Figure 30

If you are following along in the exercise workbook, you'll notice that as you pick a different month, the Month and the YTD values update. Since the formulas were designed to work with three-letter abbreviated month names, the formulas would produce an error if a spelled-out month name was entered. Thus, Data Validation is used to ensure that the user input (the month) was specified using a three-letter abbreviation.

NOTE

The purpose of this exercise is to focus on Data Validation. It is not designed to walk you through the lookup functions used. Don't worry; we'll cover lookup functions in this course so that you'll have the ability to write similar formulas.

KB

F3 is the keyboard shortcut to paste a Named Reference. It can be used to paste the name into the Source Field of Figure 29. (Be sure to precede the name with an equal sign.) It can also be used to insert names into formulas and functions.

> **NOTE**
>
> Beginning with Excel 2010, you can select the Data Validation source with your mouse even when the range is on a different worksheet. Thus, beginning in Excel 2010, you technically don't need to set up a Named Reference in order to use a range on a different worksheet. However, I believe it is still a good idea to use Named References as Data Validation List Sources. I believe that it makes the workbooks more organized and easier to maintain over time.

This exercise is important for two reasons. First, it demonstrates how two Excel features work well together. In this case, we used Named References and Data Validation. These two features are independent, but in the real world, they are often used hand-in-hand. Almost every time I use Data Validation, I first assign a name to the list of choices. Surprisingly many other features and functions work well with each other, and I'll be sure to point out future examples.

Second, this exercise is important because it illustrates a key design principle. We'll get to the complete list of key design principles shortly, but for now, just remember this: Try to anticipate how a user can break a workbook and then prevent that from happening. In this case, the formulas were only designed to evaluate three-letter abbreviated months. Since any other format would break the worksheet, we prevented the user from entering any other format with the Data Validation feature. As you design and build your workbooks, try to anticipate how your workbook can break and then figure out a way to prevent it.

LIST WITH TABLE

In the previous example, we had the user select one month from a list of months. Since no one is creating new months these days, our month list doesn't change. Jan through Dec is pretty much the permanent list. So, in our previous exercise, we didn't need to accommodate an expanding list of choices. That is, we didn't need to make it easy for someone to add a new month to the list of choices.

However, if we needed to make it easy for someone to add a choice to the list of choices, the approach demonstrated in the previous example would not work. Why? Because when a user adds a new choice under a list, even if the list is a Named Reference, the Data Validation feature does not automatically expand to include newly added items.

Can you think of any Excel feature that does automatically expand when a new item is added under the range? Yes, Tables! This example will demonstrate how to use a Table as a Data Validation List Source.

🛈 NOTE

If the user inserts a new row within the Named Reference, the name will expand and include the new row. However, if the user types a value into a cell that is under or outside of the name, the name will exclude the newly entered value.

☑ DEPENDS ON

This content depends on knowledge of Named References, discussed in Chapter 7.

☑ DEPENDS ON

This content depends on knowledge of the Tables feature, discussed in Chapter 8.

Using a Table as a source for Data Validation lists should be simple. Unfortunately, one limitation of DV is that it does not support Table names in the source field; it only supports Named References. So, what should we do? We could try setting up a custom name that refers to a Table. Can we do that? You bet.

⏵ PRACTICE

To follow along, please refer to Exercise 6 worksheet.

In this exercise, you'll allow the user to select a sales rep from a list of reps. You'll use Data Validation to provide the in-cell drop down, and you'll use a Table to store the rep list.

The first step is to create a Table with a list of reps, which should be easy for you by now. The second step is to create a custom Named Reference for the Table. In this example, the Table has only one column so you can reference the Table's name. However, if your Table had multiple columns, you would use a structured reference such as TableName[ColumnName] to identify the desired column.

If you are working along with this example, convert the range of reps to a Table and name the Table tbl_reps. Next, open the Name Manager and set up a new name (dd_reps) that refers to the Table name (tbl_reps), as shown in Figure 31 below. Be sure to precede the Table name with an equal sign (=).

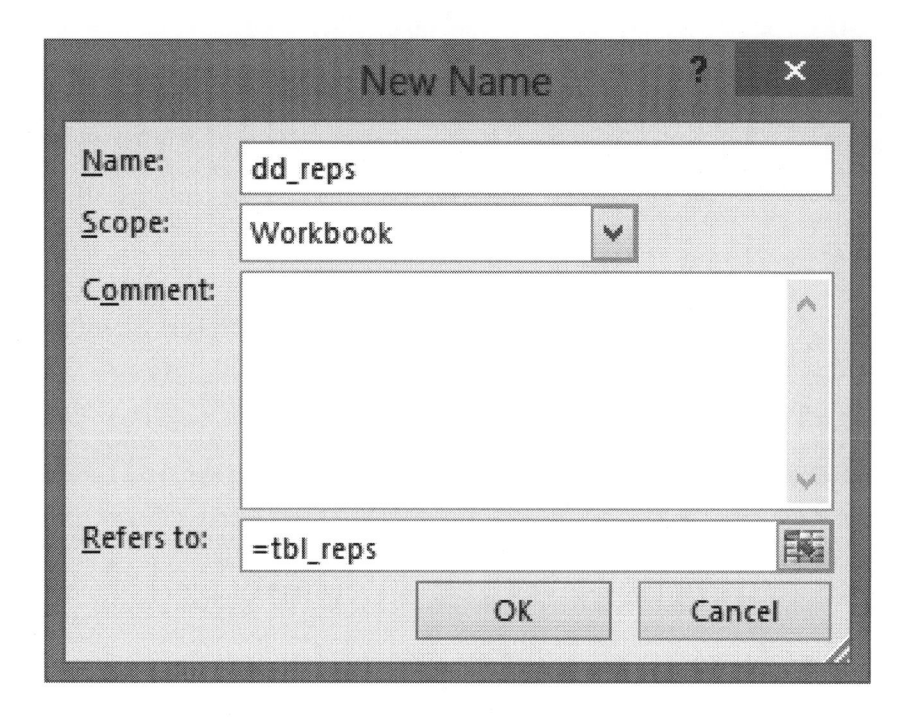

Figure 31

KB

A fast way to set up a Named Reference for the Table is by highlighting the Table first (or the selected area within the Table) and then type Alt+I, N, D (insert, name, define). (Alternatively, Alt+M, N or Ctrl+F3). You'll notice that the "Refers to" field automatically defaults to the selected range, and thus all you need to do is type in the Name.

Now that the Table has been set up and you have a Named Reference that refers to the Table, you can turn on Data Validation. Set up DV on the input cell to allow a list. The source for the list should be the Named Reference, dd_reps, as shown in Figure 32 below. Be sure to precede the name with an equal sign (=).

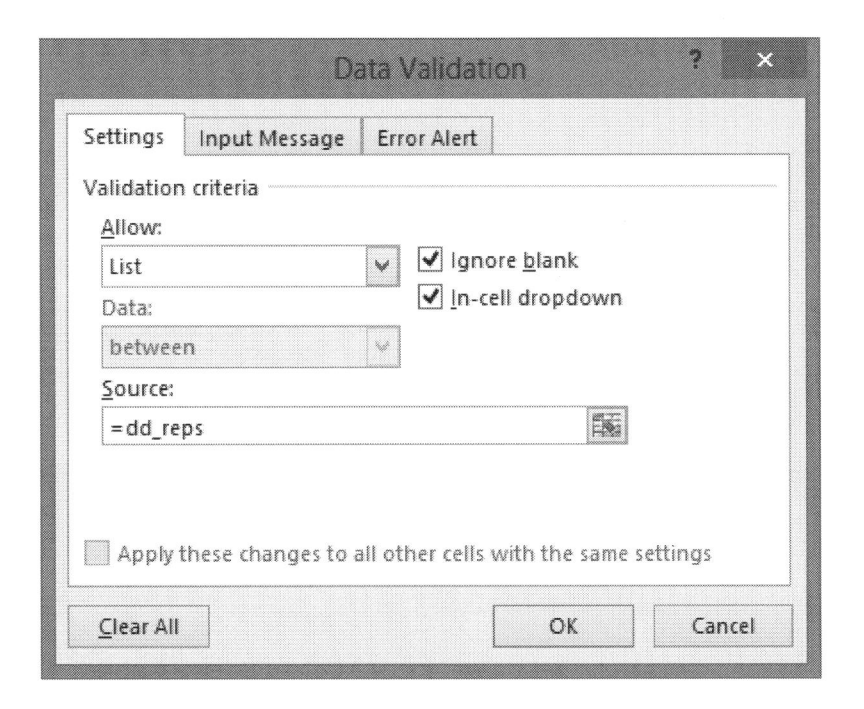

Figure 32

Ensure that the reps appear in the in-cell drop down as expected.

At last we arrive to the big moment. Add a new rep to the Table by typing the new rep under the Table. The Table should auto-expand to include this new item. Now, ensure that the new rep appears in the in-cell drop down. Did it work? Yes!

To recap, we set up a range that included a list of choices. Since we wanted the workbook to be easy to maintain, we converted the list of choices to a Table so that new choices could easily be added to the list. Since Data Validation does not support Table names as list sources, we had to work around the limitation by creating a custom name that referred to the Table name. We set up DV and used the custom name as the list source. We ensured it all worked by adding a new item to the Table and checked that the drop down included the new item. Three independent Excel features all working in harmony is a beautiful thing.

Please use this approach for all Data Validation drop down lists that you create during the remainder of our time together.

CHAPTER CONCLUSION

My goal for this chapter was to introduce Data Validation by demonstrating several practical examples. It is a powerful feature that helps us create bulletproof workbooks. When we anticipate a condition that will break our formulas, we can use Data Validation to prevent the condition. That is, we can stop users from breaking our workbooks.

> **XREF**
>
> Additional elements of Data Validation are discussed in a subsequent book.

Chapter 10: Conditional Formatting Basics

The Conditional Formatting feature allows you to control the format of a cell based on the value of the cell. This feature is useful when establishing Excel reports, KPIs, and dashboards and alerting the user to potential problems in the workbook. This chapter is meant to be a warm-up, covering the basics of conditional formatting. This concept is revisited throughout the course, and additional uses and applications will be highlighted as we proceed.

SET UP

Conditional formatting allows you to control the *format* of a cell based on the current *value* of the cell. The *format* of a cell is defined by its cell shading, font, border style, color, and so on. The *value* of a cell is determined by the current stored value or the current formula results. With Conditional Formatting, you provide formatting rules, or conditions. When the value in the cell matches a given condition, the appropriate format is applied. As the cell value changes, Excel updates the formatting appropriately. Excel continuously monitors the values of the conditionally formatted cells and updates the formatting according to the rules you've defined.

When can we use this feature? The answer is, all the time. Let's first consider using this feature to assist with reporting duties. If you ever provide reports to people, there are benefits to using this feature. One benefit is that Conditional Formatting makes it fast and easy for people to understand your reports. You see, people more easily read and understand financial and other numerical data when there is a graphical element or a picture. When Excel charts are just too big, fancy, and complicated, and you are just looking for something simple and easy, use Conditional Formatting.

Another benefit is increased efficiency. For example, let's say you prepare a report each month that requires you to highlight or format certain cells or rows. Perhaps you need to format the departments that are over budget or invoices that are very old. Rather than apply the formatting manually each month, you can delegate that task to Excel with Conditional Formatting. That way, as the values in the report change each month, Excel will automatically update the formatting according to your rules.

In addition to helping with reports that are provided to others, this feature is quite useful for internal purposes, such as error checking. With this feature, you can tell Excel to alert you to potential errors in the workbook. As a quick example, let's say you have a worksheet that contains a balance sheet, and it's terrific when the balance sheet is in balance, and assets equal liabilities and equity. But if the balance sheet is out of balance, you have a problem. Excel can alert you to this problem with the Conditional Formatting feature by changing a cell color to red, a very bright red. This is one simple example of an alert to an error condition. In a typical accountant's work, many conditions must be true for worksheets to be accurate. Other examples include when debits must equal credits, cash on the balance sheet must equal cash on the cash flow statement, and the trial balance must foot to zero.

As you can imagine, the Conditional Format is quite useful, so let's get to it.

HOW TO

The Conditional Formatting feature is actually pretty easy to use. The basic idea is to first identify the cell to be conditionally formatted. Then, define the condition(s), or rule(s). Finally, define the format to apply when the cell value meets a condition. A simple example is something like this: If the cell value equals zero, then turn the cell fill to blue. Or, if the cell value is less than zero, turn the font color to red. Let's work through this process, step by step.

To apply Conditional Formatting, simply highlight the cell or range of cells, and then activate the Conditional Format dialog box by using the following:

- RibbonUI: Home > Conditional Formatting
- MenuUI: Format > Conditional Formatting

Beginning with Excel 2007, there are many built-in rules, such as highlighting all cells greater than a value, less than a value, between two dates, above the average, within the top 10, duplicate values, and many more. Sometimes, these built-in rules are exactly what we need. However, when they are not, we'll need to create our own rules.

For the remainder of this discussion, I'll only present the RibbonUI commands since Excel 2003 didn't contain the built-in rules below. If you are following along with Excel 2003, you will be able to perform some but not all of the examples below, and be advised that the mechanics will differ.

To use a built-in rule, simply navigate to it from the Conditional Formatting Ribbon button. To set up a custom rule, activate the New Formatting Rule dialog box by navigating to:

- Home > Conditional Formatting > New Rule

To edit or delete existing rules, or to add a new rule, activate the Conditional Formatting Rules Manager dialog by navigating to the following:

- Home > Conditional Formatting > Manage Rules

There are several ways to remove Conditional Formatting from cells, but the quickest is to navigate to the following Ribbon icon:

- Home > Conditional Formatting > Clear Rules

We'll play with some of the built-in rules in this chapter, and then we'll create some custom rules in a subsequent book. At this point in our time together, I just want to cover the basics. We will explore the advanced uses of Conditional Formatting later in the course and will build on the foundations that we have learned here.

EXAMPLES

Let's work through the Conditional Formatting feature of Excel using a series of examples.

PRACTICE

To follow along, please refer to the Conditional Formatting.xlsx workbook.

VIDEO

To watch me complete the exercises, please visit the Excel University video library at www.clickconsulting.com/books.

GREATER THAN / LESS THAN

Each month, you generate a report that compares each department's actual SG&A to forecast. You are required to highlight the departments whose variance is greater than 10% of forecast, plus or minus.

Since this report is something you prepare each month, you decide to delegate the formatting task to Excel, rather than manually apply the formats. Thus, you implement Conditional Formatting.

PRACTICE

To follow along, please refer to the Exercise 1 worksheet.

First, highlight the range that you'd like to evaluate and format, which in this case, is the Variance column.

NOTE

In this chapter, the cells that are formatted are the same cells that contain the values. In a subsequent book, I'll demonstrate how to use Conditional Formatting with a formula in order to format selected cells based on the values in different cells.

Now, you'll establish a formatting rule to highlight the departments with a favorable variance; that is, a variance greater than 10%. Apply Conditional Formatting by selecting the following Ribbon button:

- Home > Conditional Formatting > Highlight Cell Rules > Greater Than

In the Greater Than dialog, enter the value (or reference) that triggers the formatting (10% in this case) and then select a built-in format style (Green Fill with Dark Green Text in this case) or a custom format from the drop down, as shown in Figure 33 below.

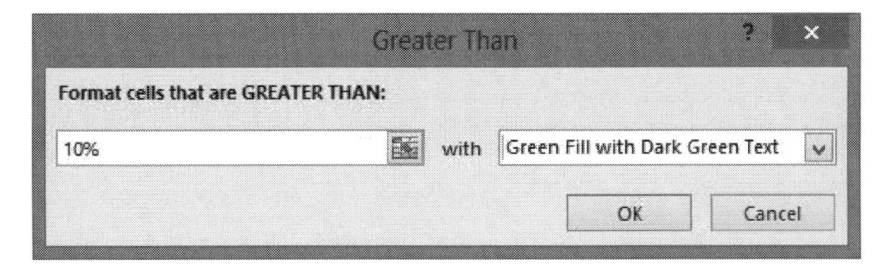

Figure 33

If this process was done properly, the cells in your worksheet that meet the condition (i.e., cells greater than 10%) will be formatted accordingly.

NOTE

If this didn't work, be sure that you selected all of the cells in the Variance column prior to setting the Conditional Formatting rules.

Next, identify the departments with large unfavorable variances, that is, variances of less than minus 10%. Highlight the Variance column, and then select the following Ribbon icon:

- Home > Conditional Formatting > Highlight Cell Rules > Less Than

In the Less Than dialog, enter the value (or reference) that triggers the formatting (-10% in this case) and then select the built-in format style (Light Red Fill with Dark Red Text in this case) or custom format from the drop down, as shown in Figure 34 below.

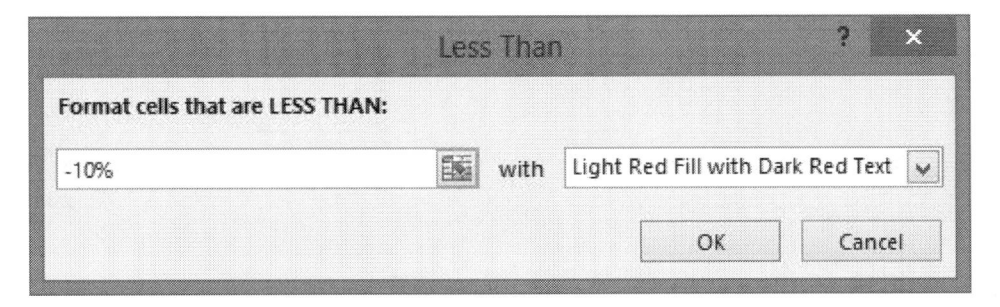

Figure 34

If this process was done correctly, the cells in the worksheet that meet the condition (i.e., cells less than -10%) will be formatted accordingly.

The best part about delegating the formatting task to Excel through the Conditional Formatting feature is that Excel will now continuously monitor the values in those cells and update the formatting accordingly. Thus, next period when the new values are entered, Excel will automatically update the formatting.

Now, that's what I'm talking about!

EQUAL TO / NOT EQUAL TO

Each month, you are required to work through the corporate cell phone bill and allocate the total expense to each department, based on the actual phone lines and minutes used for each employee. After tabulating the results, you need to enter the amounts into an Excel workbook to prepare the journal entry.

You would like to ensure that debits equal credits in this journal entry, and you'd like to have Excel alert you when the entry is out of balance. Thus, you decide to implement Conditional Formatting.

You have set up summary functions to add up total debits and total credits, and have written a formula to compute the difference between debits and credits. When the difference is equal to zero, your journal entry is in balance. When the difference does not equal zero, debits do not equal credits, and thus the journal entry is out of balance.

You decide to apply Conditional Formatting to the difference value cell, opting for green formatting when debits equal credits and red formatting when the journal entry is out of balance.

PRACTICE

To follow along, please refer to the Exercise 2 worksheet.

You select the difference value cell and then click the following Ribbon icon:

- Home > Conditional Formatting > Highlight Cell Rules > Equal To

Using the dialog box, you indicate that when the cell value is equal to zero, Excel should apply Green Fill with Dark Green Text, as shown in Figure 35 below.

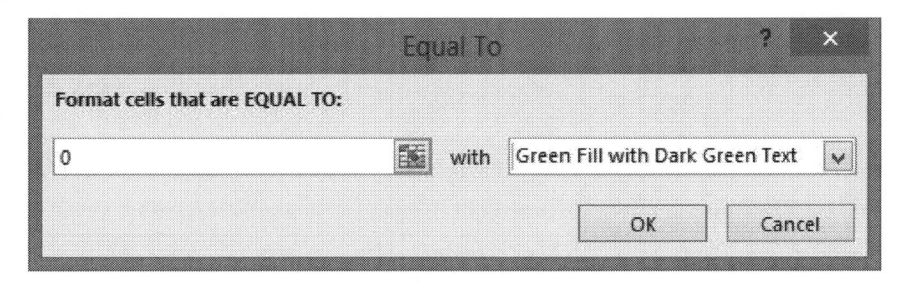

Figure 35

Next, you need to tell Excel to color the cell red when the value does not equal zero. There are at least three ways that I know of to accomplish this:

- Don't use conditional formatting
- Set up a new custom rule (instead of using a built-in rule)
- Apply two additional built-in rules, one for greater than zero and the other for less than zero

I'll chat about each of them now so that you know the options and can decide which approach you prefer. In real life, I would elect to set up a new custom rule.

Don't Use Conditional Formatting

Let's think about the way the Conditional Formatting feature works for a moment. We instruct Excel to apply a certain cell format when the cell value meets a condition. Said another way, we instruct Excel to replace the current cell format with our defined format when the cell value meets a condition. That is, manual cell formats are replaced by conditionally applied formats. This means that you can apply a manual cell format to a cell while also applying Conditional Formatting to the same cell.

Applying this knowledge to the current example, you could manually format the cell fill red. Your red fill format would exist until the value triggered the conditional green format. If you recall, you set up Conditional Formatting to fill the cell green when the value equals zero. This means that the cell fill would be red unless the value equals zero, at which time, the Conditional Formatting feature would automatically apply green.

So to recap, our current task is to fill the cell with green when the value equals zero, and fill the cell with red when the value does not equal zero. As you can see, we can use a simple technique to accomplish this task. We simply format the cell red, and then set up one conditional format rule to apply green when the cell value equals zero.

This technique was especially important in earlier versions of Excel, such as Excel 2003 and earlier, because we were limited to only three Conditional Formatting rules. This technique allowed us to create four different formats (the manual format plus the three conditional formats). In recent versions of Excel, such as Excel 2007 and later, Microsoft removed the limit. Since we can now define an unlimited number of rules, this technique is not as important these days.

Personally, I prefer to define the formats explicitly using the Conditional Formatting feature and most likely would not choose this technique in practice. However, it is one option. Let's look at the next approach, the one I would mostly likely use in the real world.

Set up a New Rule

In practice, I would set up a new rule that tells Excel to format the cell red when the cell value does not equal zero. However, since this requires a custom rule rather than one of the built-in shortcut rules, I demonstrate this technique along with other advanced applications in a subsequent book.

XREF
Setting up custom rules is discussed in a subsequent book.

Apply Two Additional Rules

In this chapter we are temporarily limited to using only the built-in shortcut rules and will simply apply two additional Conditional Formatting rules: one rule to format the cell red when the value is greater than zero, and another rule to format the cell red when the value is less than zero.

This is done in two steps. First, highlight the cell and then select the following Ribbon icon:

- Home > Conditional Formatting > Cell Value Rules > Greater Than

Use the Greater Than dialog to format the cell red when the value is greater than zero. Next, apply an additional rule by selecting the following Ribbon Icon:

- Home > Conditional Formatting > Cell Value Rules > Less Than

Use the Less Than dialog to apply red when the cell value is less than zero.

Now, if you have properly set up all three rules (green when zero, red when greater than zero, and red when less than zero), the difference value will equal zero and have green cell formatting applied when your telephone expense journal entry is in balance. When your journal entry is out of balance, the difference value will not equal zero and will have red cell formatting applied.

> **NOTE**
>
> This is a simple form of error checking. We'll develop a more formal structure and explore more sophisticated formulas for error checking as we proceed through this course.

DUPLICATE VALUES

Beginning with Excel 2007, the Conditional Formatting feature has a built-in rule to highlight duplicate values. This can be a useful tool when you want a quick way to search a list for duplicates.

> **PRACTICE**
>
> To follow along, please refer to the Exercise 3 worksheet.

To apply this formatting rule, simply highlight the range first and then select the following Ribbon command:

- Home > Conditional Formatting > Highlight Cell Rules > Duplicate Values

From the Duplicate Values dialog box, select Duplicate or Unique values (Duplicate in this case) and then select a built-in or custom format. Click OK to apply the formatting rule, and, if done properly, the cells with duplicate values will be identified through the cell formatting. If the values change, the formatting will be updated automatically.

> **NOTE**
>
> When you select multiple columns and apply this format, each column is independently examined for duplicate values. A duplicate is defined as any value that appears more than once in the column (regardless of the other values in the row). To be clear, this feature will highlight check number 1000 if 1000 appears more than once in the column, regardless of any other values in the row such as the amount.

DATA BARS

As part of your monthly reporting package, you are required to submit a Sales by Rep summary. You are exploring ways to make your reports easier to read, so you are playing with the various graphical features of Excel. You know that people can grasp numerical data more easily when it is presented graphically, so you are making a concerted effort to add a graphical element to your deliverables.

A traditional chart is not a good fit in this case due to a handful of constraints, including space limitations. Thus, you'd like to see if there is a feature in Excel that can simulate a chart in a smaller, more compact way. One of the features you consider is Conditional Formatting with Data Bars.

> **XREF**
>
> Sparklines, a feature rolled out with Excel 2010, is another option worth considering. Sparklines are essentially one-cell charts and are discussed at length in a subsequent book.

> **PRACTICE**
>
> To follow along, please refer the Exercise 4 worksheet.

Start by highlighting the cells you want to conditionally format, in this case, the Amount column. Next, navigate to the following Ribbon icon:

- Home > Conditional Formatting > Data Bars

Pick your preferred format color and style, and, if all goes well, you'll see data bars in the cells, as shown in Figure 36 below.

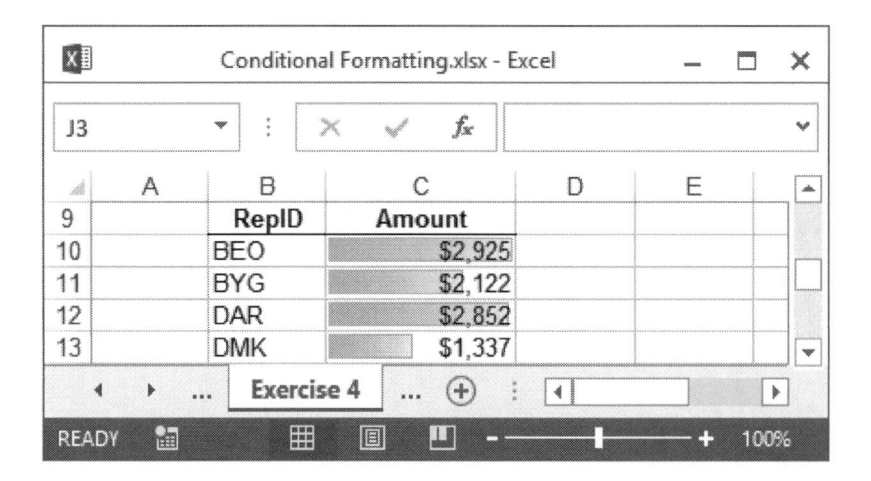

Figure 36

This feature attempts to graphically represent the relative values within the range. The largest number in the range is shaded completely, and a number 50% of the largest number is shaded halfway, and so on. This is a terrific way to quickly add a graphical touch to your data-intensive reports.

As you know, once you define the rules, you don't need to redefine them next month. When the cell values change, the formatting will automatically adjust.

ICON SETS

Each month you prepare an inventory turnover report as part of your reporting package. Inventory items with high turnover are the highest selling items and thus have little risk of accruing excess inventory. However, those items with a slower turnover are more likely to become a financial risk because they are more likely to accrue excess inventory or become obsolete. Management wants to keep on top of these items and address them in a timely manner, perhaps by offering discounts or discontinuing them.

You want to make your standard inventory turnover report easier to read, so you decide to add a graphical element. You decide to use the Icon Sets style within Conditional Formatting.

PRACTICE

To follow along, please refer to the Exercise 5 worksheet.

Highlight the range and then navigate to the following Ribbon icon:

- Home > Conditional Formatting > Icon Sets

Select the style of icons, and Excel will apply the icon sets accordingly, as illustrated in Figure 37 below.

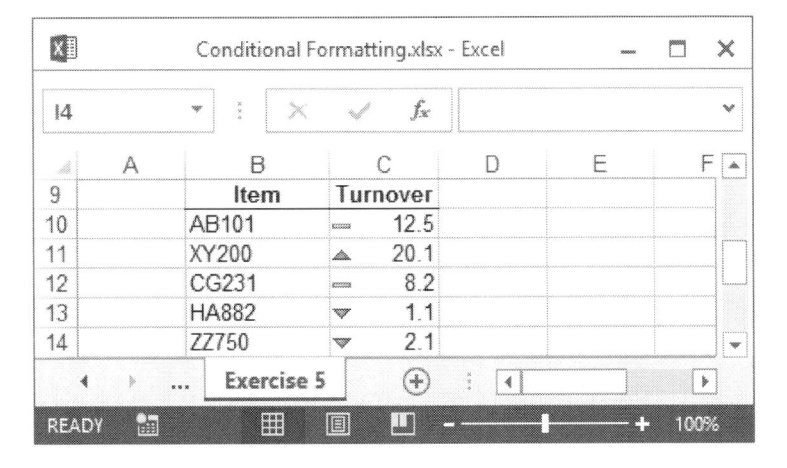

Figure 37

The math used by the Conditional Formatting feature is simple. If you select an icon set with three icons, then the range is divided into three equal sections (0 to 1/3, 1/3 to 2/3, and 2/3 to 1). Excel then applies an icon for the cells that fall into each of the three ranges. Four icons are split into fourths, and five icons are split into fifths.

> **NOTE**
>
> The default icon rules can be edited from within the Conditional Formatting Rules Manager.

Icon sets are certainly an easy way to add a graphical element to your reports. Consider using this feature when you deliver numbers to others. Icon sets will make your numbers easier to read and understand.

CHAPTER CONCLUSION

As you can tell, we've only covered a portion of all of the built-in rules. Please feel free to experiment with the other built-in rules. We'll circle back to Conditional Formatting later, highlighting some additional uses and applications.

> **XREF**
>
> Further uses of Conditional Formatting are reviewed in a subsequent book.

Chapter 11: Better Summing

What is your most frequently used worksheet function?

Was your answer the SUM function? If so, you are probably not alone. Although I can't find any evidence or proof online, I would guess that the SUM function is the most commonly used Excel function of all time.

But, it shouldn't be.

There is a function in Excel that is far better for summing than the SUM function. In fact, I use it instead of the SUM function almost all of the time. That is, I rarely use the SUM function in my workbooks. So, what is the function that sums better than the SUM function?

It is with great privilege that I introduce the SUBTOTAL function.

Let's discuss the SUBTOTAL worksheet function now. To be clear, I'm not talking about the Subtotal *feature* of Excel, I'm talking about the SUBTOTAL *function*.

XREF
The subtotal *feature* is discussed at length in a subsequent book.

SET UP

Let's start by answering the burning question: "Why is the SUBTOTAL function better than the SUM function?"

To be clear, when I state that the SUBTOTAL function is better than the SUM function, I really mean that for accountants, the SUBTOTAL function is better most of the time. There are times when the SUM function is a better fit, however, it is often more efficient to use the SUBTOTAL function.

I used to rely on the SUM function to add ranges in my workbooks. About 15 years ago, Wayne showed me the SUBTOTAL function, and I've been using it ever since (Thanks, Wayne!).

Described as succinctly as possible, here is why the SUBTOTAL function is better than the SUM function for accountants: The SUBTOTAL function excludes other SUBTOTAL functions in its range.

I'll say it once again, this time with feeling: *the SUBTOTAL function excludes other SUBTOTAL functions in its sum range*.

If the power of this hasn't quite hit you yet, that is ok. We'll work through some exercises that will help to illustrate.

HOW TO

The SUBTOTAL function has two function arguments. The first function argument allows you to tell the SUBTOTAL function the type of math to apply to the range. The second argument is the range.

The Excel developers wanted this worksheet function to be flexible. Beyond adding the values in a range, they wanted the function to handle other calculations, such as compute the average of a range or find the maximum value in a range.

We essentially tell the function the type of math (e.g., sum, average, or max) through the first function argument. If we want to add up the range, then we use a code for sum. If we want to compute an average of the range, we use a code for average.

In my workbooks, I use the SUBTOTAL function to add numbers in a range, so I use code 9 for the first function argument. 9 is the code for sum. It is the only code that I have memorized, and it is the only one I use.

The syntax for the function follows:

```
=SUBTOTAL(function_num, ref1, [ref2], …)
```

Where:

- **function_num** is the function number (see Table 1 below)

- **ref1** is the reference (range, cell, value) to subtotal
- **[ref2]** is an optional additional reference (range, cell, value)
- ... up to 254 additional references

A partial list of the codes is presented below for reference.

Code	Function
1	Average
2	Count
...	
4	Max
...	
9	Sum

Table 1

> **NOTE**
>
> For a complete list, please use the Excel help system.

The function to add the values in cells A1 through A10 follows:

```
=SUBTOTAL(9,A1:A10)
```

Where:

- **9** is the code for sum (i.e., add)
- **A1:A10** is the range to, in this case, sum

The SUBTOTAL function above would exclude from its result any other SUBTOTAL functions that existed in cells A1:A10. It excludes other SUBTOTAL functions in its range from its result.

Now, let's have some trick questions. Ready? OK, the first trick question is this: Does the SUBTOTAL function exclude other subtotals that were computed with the SUM function? The answer is no, it does not exclude SUM functions; the SUBTOTAL function includes SUM functions in its result. The SUBTOTAL function only excludes other SUBTOTAL *functions*. Thus, be sure to use the SUBTOTAL function to compute the subtotals and the grand total.

Here is the second trick question. If you used a SUBTOTAL function for a subtotal, but then used a SUM function for the grand total, would the SUM function exclude the SUBTOTAL function?

The answer is no, it would not exclude it. The SUM function doesn't exclude any other functions; it includes everything in the range. So, be sure to use the SUBTOTAL function to compute subtotals and the grand total.

I apologize for taking so many words to drive the point home, but I just want to be crystal clear on the usefulness of the SUBTOTAL function, as we'll be using this function throughout the remaining workbooks and exercises presented in this course.

Let's go ahead and play with this function using a few exercises.

KB

In versions of Excel 2007 and onward, you can use the auto-complete feature to help enter the function. Start in a cell and type the equal sign. Then, begin by typing the first few letters of the function name. When you see the function in the auto-complete list, simply use the down and up Arrows on your keyboard to select it. Then use the Tab key on your keyboard to enter the function name into the cell.

NOTE

Beyond the list presented in Table 1 above, there are additional function codes for the first argument. Codes 1 through 11 represent basic math functions. Codes 101 through 111 represent the same math functions, but have different cell inclusion rules. Codes 1 through 11 tell the SUBTOTAL function to include all cells in the range except for cells in rows that have been hidden by a Filter. Codes 101 through 111 tell the function to include all cells in the range except for cells in rows that have been hidden by a Filter, manually hidden, or hidden with the Outline feature. This is summarized in Table 2 below.

	Codes 1 to 11	Codes 101 to 111
Visible rows	INCLUDE	INCLUDE
Hidden by Filter	EXCLUDE	EXCLUDE
Hidden manually	INCLUDE	EXCLUDE
Hidden with Outline feature	INCLUDE	EXCLUDE

Table 2

To recap, Codes 1 through 11 will automatically exclude from its result any rows hidden by a Filter. Codes 101 through 111 exclude cells from hidden rows, regardless of how the rows were hidden (manually, Outline group, or Filter).

XREF

The SUBTOTAL function is revisited in the auto-filter chapter in a subsequent book where we explore how it excludes hidden rows in filtered data regions.

EXAMPLES

This function will be illustrated with several examples. It is my goal that you'll be absolutely comfortable using this function after you work through these examples. My hope is that you will integrate this function into your workbooks and consider using it as a replacement for the SUM function.

PRACTICE

To follow along, please refer to Subtotal Function.xlsx.

VIDEO

To watch me complete the exercises, please visit the Excel University video library at www.clickconsulting.com/books.

BALANCE SHEET

Let's start with the most basic financial report that there is: a balance sheet. Balance sheets have various subtotals: for example, the Fixed Assets subtotal. Balance sheets also have grand totals: for example, Total Assets. Reports that contain both subtotals and grand totals are perfect candidates for the SUBTOTAL function. Indeed, this implies that most reports you work on will be good candidates for the SUBTOTAL function.

PRACTICE

To follow along, please refer to the Exercise 1 worksheet.

A fairly common approach used to create a balance sheet (and many other reports) is to use the SUM function for all subtotal cells, such as the Fixed Assets subtotal. This is illustrated in Figure 38 below.

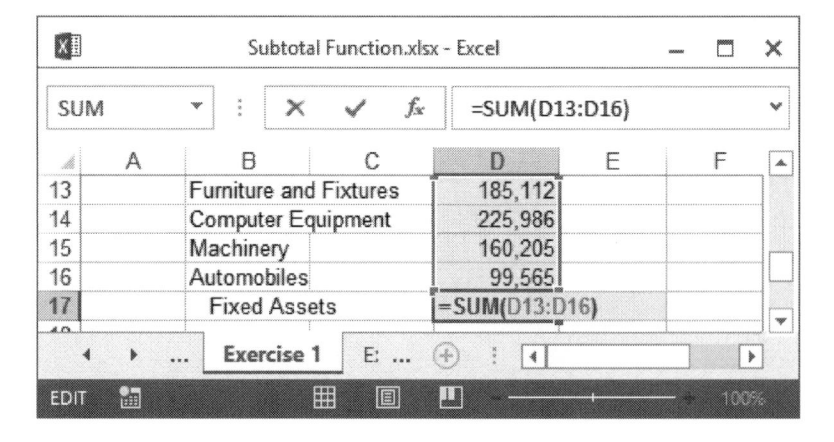

Figure 38

With this approach, computing a grand total such as Total Assets requires a formula that references each individual cell to be included in the total. In other words, you have to pick and choose the cells to include in Total Assets, as illustrated in Figure 39 below.

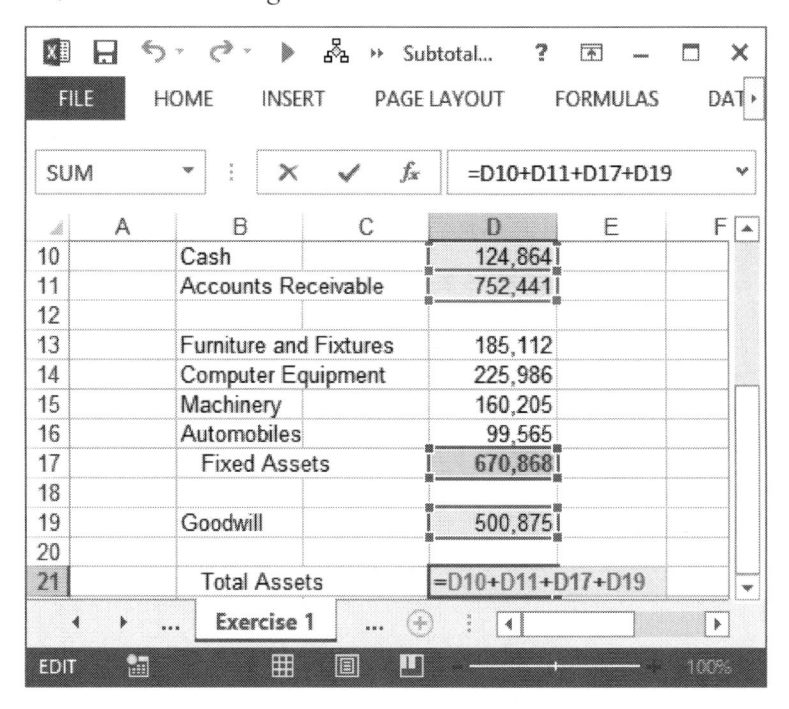

Figure 39

And that, my friend, is a fairly common approach used in balance sheets, financial reports, operational reports, and pretty much most other reports. So, what's wrong with that?

That approach is terrible. (No offense.) That approach is error prone and inefficient. Why? It is error prone because if a user inserts Inventory under Accounts Receivable, the Total Assets formula will improperly exclude Inventory. That is, the balance sheet won't foot, which is an error. That means that the user will need to manually rewrite or update the Total Assets formula, and that is inefficient.

So what is a better approach? What is better summing? It is, of course, the SUBTOTAL function. Why? Because the SUBTOTAL function excludes other SUBTOTAL functions in its range.

When we properly set up the balance sheet, we can use the SUBTOTAL function to compute Total Assets by specifying the whole range of assets. This means that any new rows inserted into the balance sheet (such as Inventory) will automatically be included in the Total Assets value. This approach, as you can imagine, reduces errors because new items are automatically included in the grand total. It also improves efficiency because it reduces the need to rewrite or update the grand total formula.

Let's see how to use the SUBTOTAL approach in our balance sheet. First, we use a SUBTOTAL function to compute the Fixed Assets subtotal, as shown in Figure 40 below.

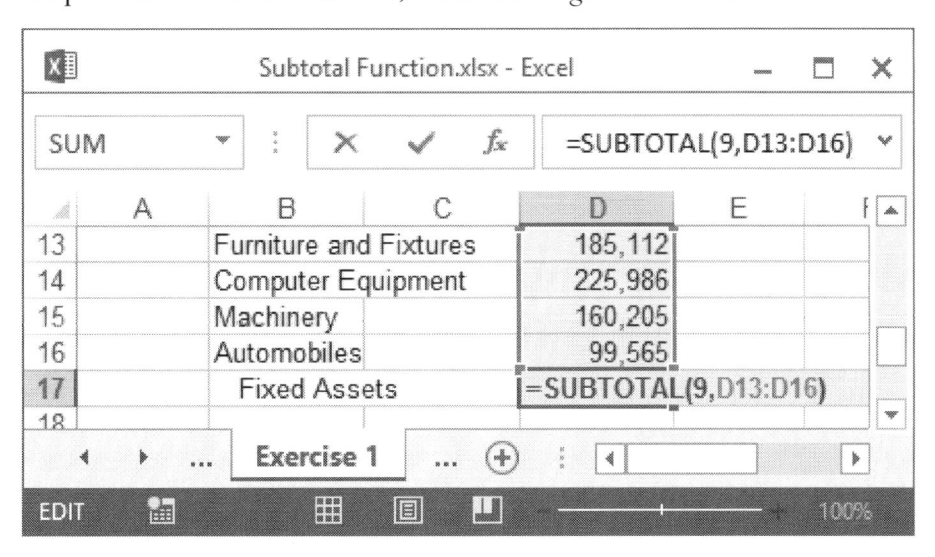

Figure 40

Since a SUBTOTAL function is used to compute the Fixed Assets subtotal, it means you can use another SUBTOTAL function to compute Total Assets, as shown in Figure 41 below.

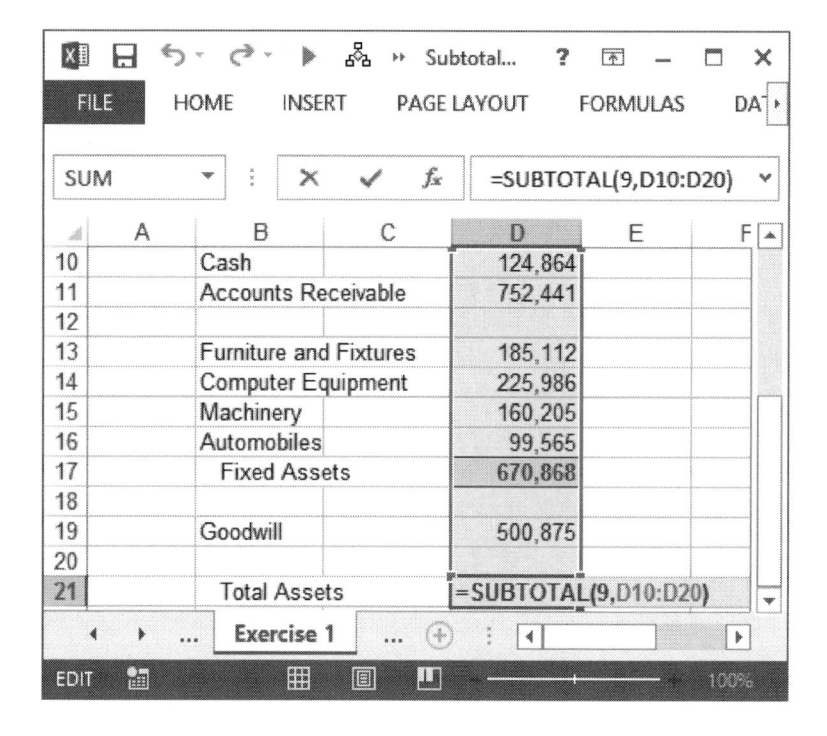

[Screenshot of Excel showing a balance sheet with Cash, Accounts Receivable, Furniture and Fixtures, Computer Equipment, Machinery, Automobiles, Fixed Assets subtotal, Goodwill, and Total Assets with formula =SUBTOTAL(9,D10:D20)]

Figure 41

Now, as you can see, since the Total Assets function includes the entire Assets range from D10:D20, any new assets added within that range will automatically be included. Since we used a SUBTOTAL function to compute the Fixed Assets subtotal, it will be properly excluded from the Total.

This is the correct approach, and is the one we'll use from this day forward when designing financial statements and reports that have subtotals.

The key thing to remember: Use the SUBTOTAL function to compute both the subtotals and the grand total. Let's explore some other areas where the SUBTOTAL function is useful.

DEPARTMENT REPORT

In this exercise, you'll have the opportunity to set up several SUBTOTAL functions in the context of a department report.

PRACTICE

To follow along, please refer to the Exercise 2 worksheet.

Each department belongs to an organizational group. It is your job to compute subtotals for each group and then compute a grand total for the company. You decide to implement the SUBTOTAL function.

You use the SUBTOTAL function to compute all group subtotals. You are then free to use the SUBTOTAL function for the grand total. Since the SUBTOTAL function excludes other SUBTOTAL functions in the range, your results are accurate.

The completed report is shown in Figure 42 below.

	DeptID	Department	Q1	Q2	Q3	Q4
		Department Report				
	100	Corporate	$149,617	$255,652	$219,500	$349,062
	101	Accounting	$359,334	$194,638	$456,301	$205,269
	102	HR	$491,038	$468,210	$367,590	$169,858
		Group Subtotal	$999,989	$918,500	$1,043,391	$724,189
	200	Operations	$239,752	$392,538	$283,061	$336,198
	202	Research	$101,058	$399,246	$367,008	$188,655
	206	Manufacturing	$357,508	$192,768	$106,349	$237,665
		Group Subtotal	$698,318	$984,552	$756,418	$762,518
	301	Sales	$298,198	$471,041	$167,329	$137,880
	305	Marketing	$397,510	$256,609	$356,504	$499,822
		Group Subtotal	$695,708	$727,650	$523,833	$637,702
	400	Logistics	$457,376	$320,175	$289,996	$163,913
	410	IT	$276,611	$105,785	$365,720	$483,014
	420	Warehouse	$398,523	$291,788	$266,605	$167,764
		Group Subtotal	$1,132,510	$717,748	$922,321	$814,691
		Company Total	=SUBTOTAL(9,D11:D29)			$2,939,100

Formula bar: =SUBTOTAL(9,D11:D29)

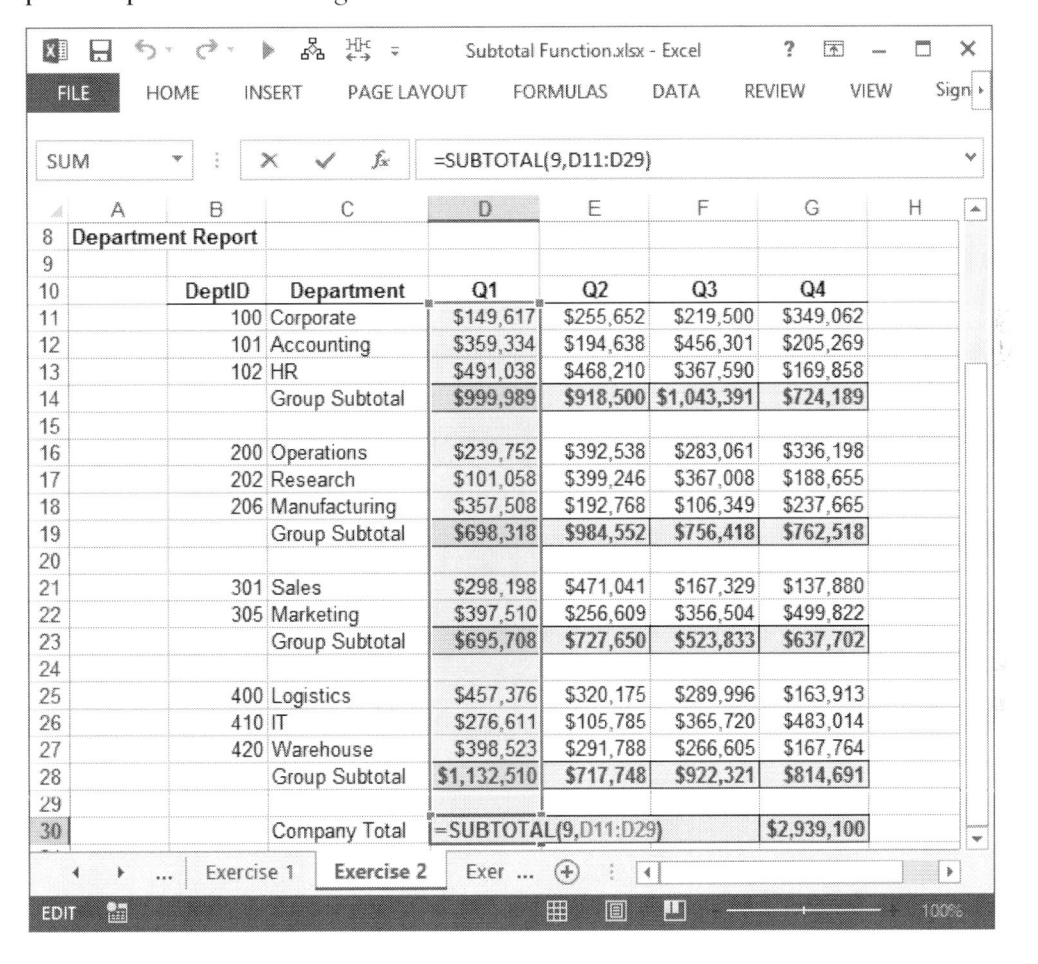

Figure 42

SG&A

In this exercise, you'll use the SUBTOTAL function to tabulate an SG&A report.

PRACTICE

To follow along, please refer to the Exercise 3 worksheet.

Insert the SUBTOTAL function at each of the subtotal lines and then use the SUBTOTAL function again to compute the total SG&A, as shown in Figure 43 below.

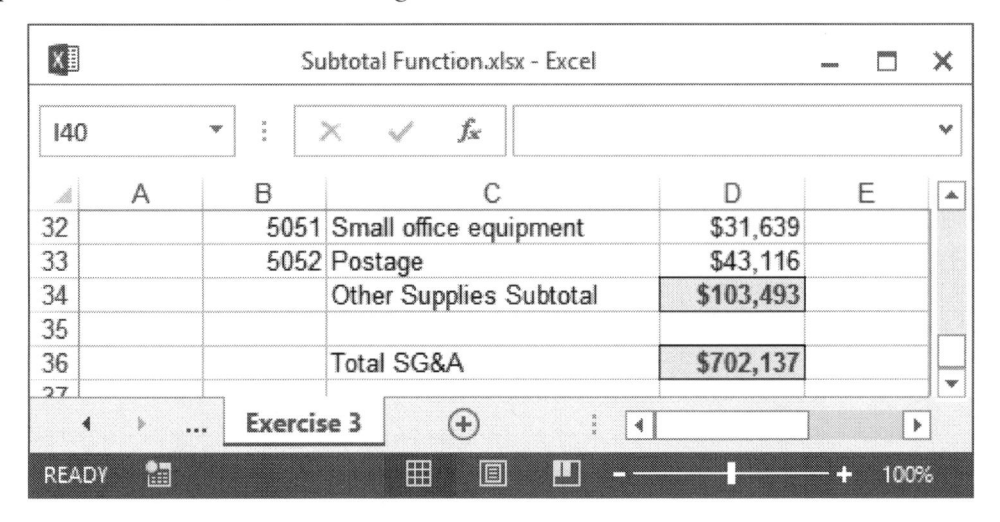

	A	B	C	D	E
32		5051	Small office equipment	$31,639	
33		5052	Postage	$43,116	
34			Other Supplies Subtotal	$103,493	
35					
36			Total SG&A	$702,137	

Figure 43

I hope that by working through the examples, you've gained comfort using the SUBTOTAL function and will begin to use it in your workbooks.

CHAPTER CONCLUSION

If you didn't know about the SUBTOTAL function before this course, I'm excited that you know about it now and can begin to benefit from its power and flexibility. In the wise words of Fergie, "If you didn't know that, well, baby, now you know now." Moreover, now that you know about this function, you can implement it into your workbooks to make them more accurate and efficient.

I feel so strongly about using the SUBTOTAL function as a replacement for the SUM function, that I wrote an article about it called "Sum No More." See the Additional Resources section below for more information. Please consider using the SUBTOTAL function in your workbooks starting today. Now, go, and sum no more!

ADDITIONAL RESOURCES

For additional information on the SUBTOTAL function, please refer to my article **"SUM() No More,"** published in the June 2011 Wisconsin Institute of CPA's *Calliope*, available online at clickconsulting.com or wicpa.org.

This piece walks through the SUBTOTAL function and provides additional information.

Chapter 12: Skinny Row

Most of the exercise workbooks that we've used thus far have contained a glaring inefficiency. I'm so excited that we are now going to discuss the Skinny Row Technique, so that we can use it in the remaining exercise workbooks. The Skinny Row Technique helps to improve efficiency and reduce errors in your workbooks.

SET UP

You longtime Excel users will know the answer to the following question: If you have a region of data, and then put a SUM function directly under the region (adjacent to it), what happens to your SUM function when you insert a new row between the data region and the SUM function? That is, what happens if you insert a new row at the location represented by the arrow in Figure 44 below?

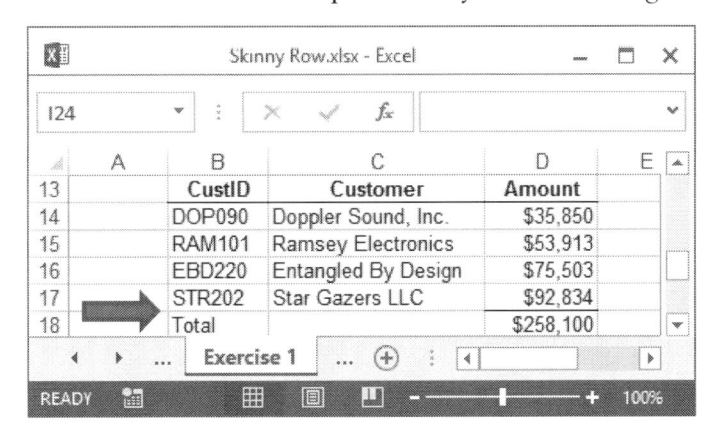

Figure 44

Does the SUM function automatically adjust itself to include the newly inserted row? It does not, as illustrated in Figure 45 below.

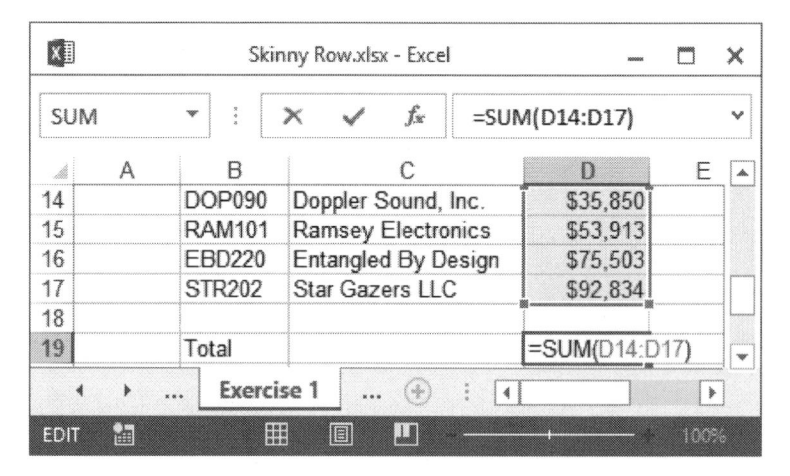

Figure 45

This results in workbooks that are error-prone and inefficient. They are error prone because the new row is improperly excluded from the total and inefficient because you need to manually rewrite or update the sum function to include the new row in the total. To make our workbooks more accurate and efficient, we'll use the Skinny Row Technique to address this issue.

> **NOTE**
>
> It is important to note that Microsoft has addressed this issue over the years. As illustrated above, after you insert a new row, the formula does not update itself to include the new row. However, once you enter a value into the new cell, Excel will update the formula to include the new row. This is excellent. Another example of how this has been addressed is that when a formula does not include adjacent data, an error alert will appear in the cell. However, maybe out of habit, or my own personal level of comfort, I prefer to use the Skinny Row Technique, as I've found it to be absolutely bulletproof.

HOW TO

The Skinny Row Technique is not a feature or a function in Excel; it is simply a technique. The Skinny Row is any blank row between the data region and the formula row. The row height is decreased so that it is *skinny*. I typically use a row height of 4, but you can also use other values, such as 3, 2, 1 or .75. Since the row is skinny, it is not noticeable on printed versions of the sheet. After you create the Skinny

Row, you must write your formula to include it. That is, the function that computes the Total needs to include the Skinny Row. Notice the Skinny Row between the data and the formula in Figure 46 below.

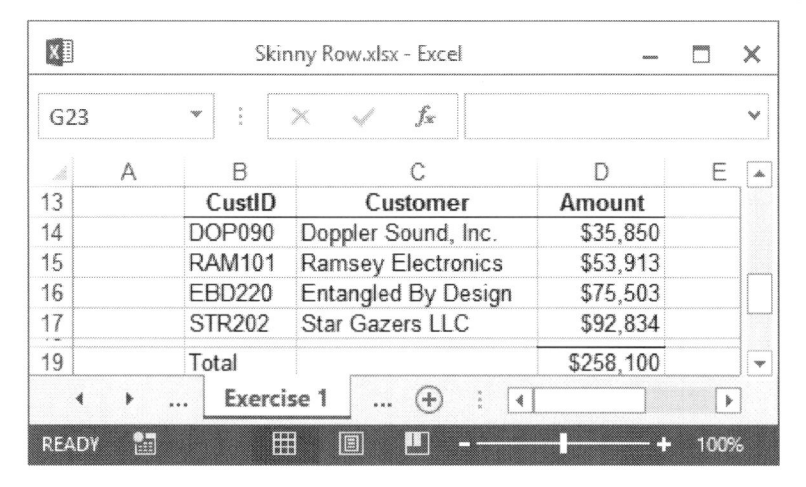

Figure 46

When a user selects the Skinny Row and inserts a new row, the formula will automatically include the new row. Essentially, you are inserting a new row within the sum range rather than under the sum range.

It is important to point out again that the sum formula must include the Skinny Row for this technique to be effective, as shown in Figure 47 below.

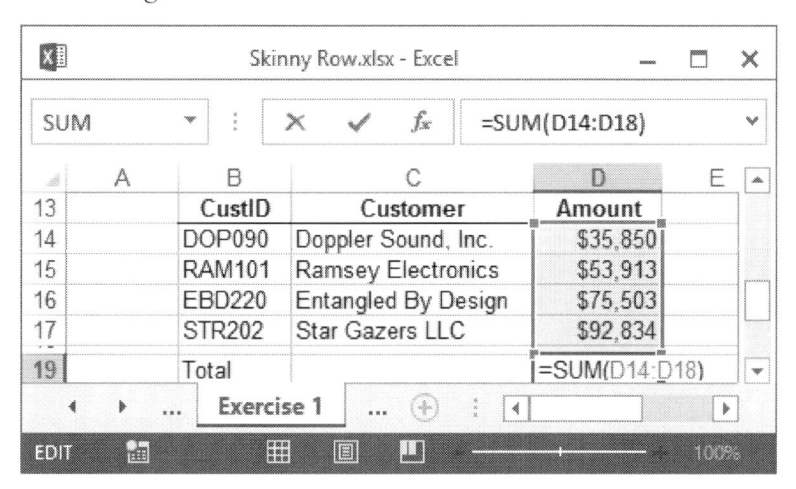

Figure 47

There are additional benefits to using a Skinny Row. For example, the cell formatting (perhaps a bottom border) can be placed in the Skinny Row rather than in the last data row. That way when you insert new rows, the formatting does not need to be adjusted. Additionally, when using keyboard shortcuts to travel down, you'll stop at the Skinny Row. Plus, when you fill formulas down using the double-click shortcut, the formula will stop before the total row.

Now, does setting up a Skinny Row take an extra step when creating the workbook? Yes. Does that extra step take time? Yes. Therefore, the implementation of this technique takes longer in the short term. However, the implementation of this technique saves time in the long term, since the workbook will be more efficient to maintain on an ongoing basis and will have fewer errors. So, would I use this technique on one-time use workbooks? Maybe. But would I use this technique on workbooks I use on a recurring basis? Absolutely!

EXAMPLES

Now, let's get some experience implementing the Skinny Row Technique with several exercises.

PRACTICE

To follow along, please refer to the Skinny Row.xlsx workbook.

VIDEO

To watch me complete the exercises, please visit the Excel University video library at www.clickconsulting.com/books.

CUSTOMER SALES

In this exercise, you'll be summarizing customer sales data.

PRACTICE

To follow along, please refer to the Exercise 1 worksheet.

You need to write a function to compute the sum of the Amount column. Now, before you write the function to compute the sum, change the height of the row immediately under the data region. For our purposes, try a height of 4, but you can use other heights if you prefer. There are several ways to change the row height of the active cell or cells. One quick way is by using the following command:

- RibbonUI: Home > Format > Row Height

- MenuUI: Format > Rows > Height

KB

Here is the keyboard sequence I use to change the row height. I navigate to any cell in the row. Then, I use Alt+O, R, E, (f<u>o</u>rmat, <u>r</u>ow, and h<u>e</u>ight). Then, I type 4 into the Row Height dialog box, and press Enter.

You should end up with the worksheet as shown in Figure 48 below.

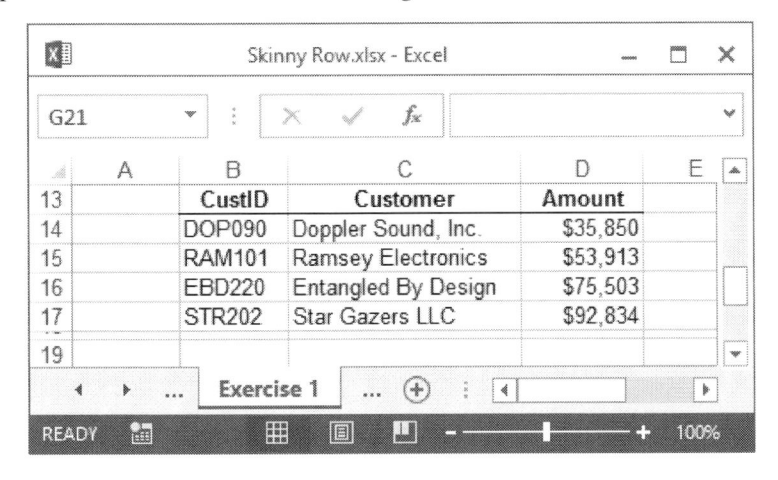

Figure 48

Now, go ahead and write the sum formula (SUM, SUBTOTAL, or other function), and be sure that the function's argument includes the Skinny Row, as shown in Figure 49 below.

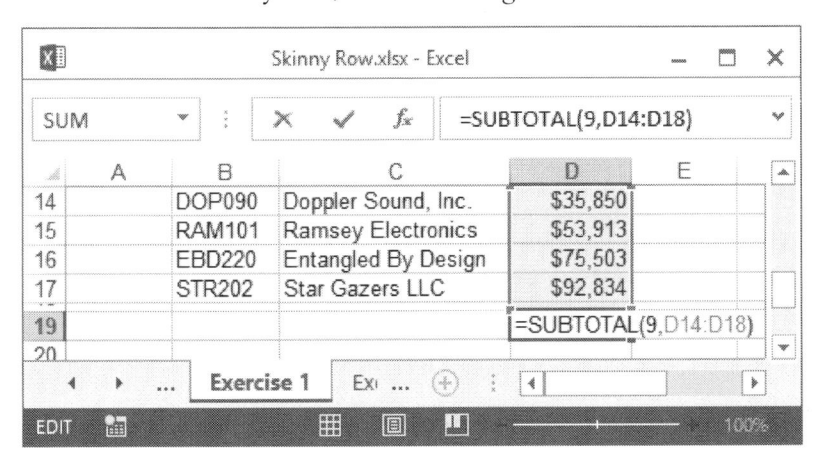

Figure 49

Chapter 12: Skinny Row   **125**

Now, insert a new row between the data region and the formula row by selecting the Skinny Row and then inserting a new row.

> **KB**
>
> Here is the keyboard shortcut to insert a new row. Select any cell in the Skinny Row and then press Alt I, R (insert, row). Alternatively, to use keyboard shortcuts to navigate the Ribbon, you would use Alt H, I, R (home, insert, row).

Check your formula to ensure that it automatically includes the new row, as shown in Figure 50 below.

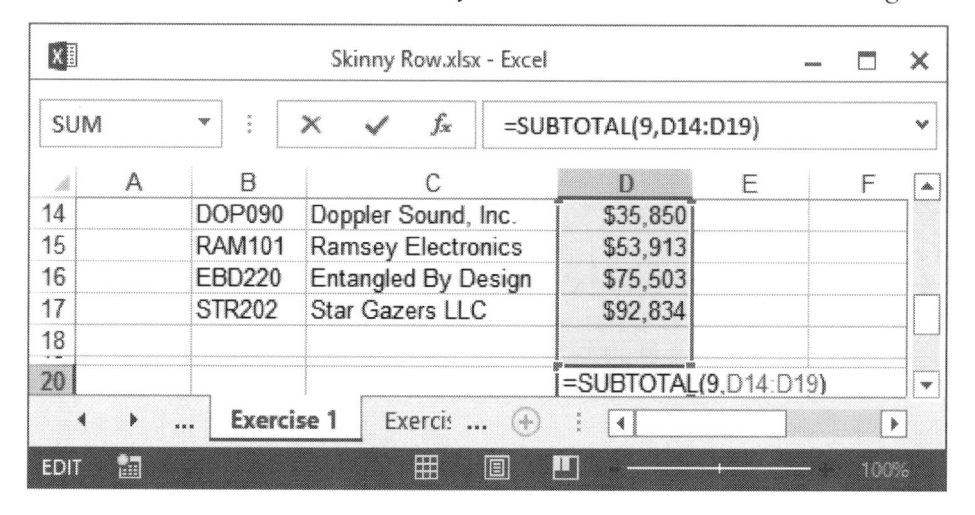

Figure 50

So that, my friend, is the basic idea behind the Skinny Row Technique. Let's now see how I would have built some of the previous workbooks used in this course with the Skinny Row.

DEPARTMENT REPORT

For this exercise, let's revisit the structure of a worksheet we used previously.

> **PRACTICE**
>
> To follow along, please refer to the Exercise 2 worksheet.

You may recall this sheet from our work on the SUBTOTAL function. The approach I used to set up the structure of this worksheet was incorrect. Why? Because there are no Skinny Rows, and therefore updating and maintaining this workbook over time is inaccurate and inefficient.

So, in this case we need to update the structure by inserting Skinny Rows before all Group Subtotal rows and before the Company Total row. Now that the Skinny Rows are in place, you can feel free to write the required SUBTOTAL functions to compute the subtotals and company total.

Now if you insert a new department into the report, the SUBTOTAL functions will include it. Mission accomplished.

END OF DATA REGIONS

Beyond using a Skinny Row between data regions and formulas as we've done thus far, Skinny Rows are a convenient way to designate the end of a data region when formulas reference it.

DEPENDS ON

The content in this section requires knowledge of Named References (discussed in Chapter 7) and Tables (discussed in Chapter 8).

This technique is not required, of course, when data regions are converted to Tables. However, when a data region is not converted to a Table, and you have formulas that reference the data region, it is important to denote the end of the data region with a Skinny Row and to make sure that the formulas include the Skinny Row. The Skinny Row provides a visual reminder that there are formulas that reference the data region.

PRACTICE

To follow along, please refer to the Exercise 3 worksheet.

In this example, we'll revisit one of our previous exercises. When we were working with Named References, we had an exercise that called for us to name a column so that we could write a SUM function that would easily sum the column. This formula summed a single column within the data region, and it is important to realize that the Skinny Row Technique is useful even when only a single column is used in formulas. That is, even if you don't name the entire data range, and you only name a single column, you can still use the Skinny Row Technique to mark the lower bound of the name's reference.

When you complete the exercise this time around, set up a Skinny Row under the data region. When you create the Named Reference for the Amount column, be sure it includes the Skinny Row. Set up the SUM function to sum the Named Reference. Did it work? Great! Now, whenever you open this sheet, you'll see your Skinny Row and you'll know that a formula somewhere refers to this data region, and thus, you'll insert new rows above the Skinny Row.

As you can imagine, this technique will help to reduce errors in your worksheets (since new data will properly be included in the formulas) and will improve your efficiency (since you won't need to track down and update formulas).

SKINNY COLUMNS

You can just as easily set up a Skinny Column to denote the right edge of a data region. This is important when you add new columns that need to be included in your formulas. I personally don't use Skinny Columns nearly as often as Skinny Rows, mainly because the workbooks I work with require data to be added to new rows, rather than new columns.

PRACTICE

To follow along, please refer to the Exercise 4 worksheet.

In this exercise, you are working on a report, and you anticipate that over the next several months you'll be adding columns. Specifically, you'll be adding an additional column for each month. Since you anticipate that you'll be adding new columns, and you have a Total formula that operates on the data region, you decide to set up a Skinny Column between the data and the formula columns by using the following command:

- RibbonUI: Home > Format > Column Width
- MenuUI: Format > Columns > Width

This is represented in Figure 51 below by column G.

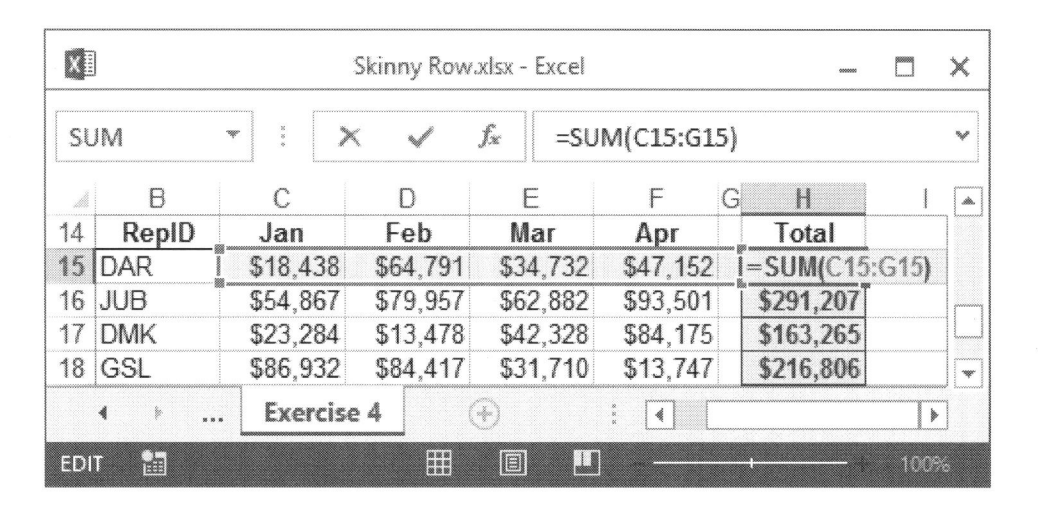

Figure 51

> **KB**
>
> Here is the keyboard sequence I use to change the column width. I navigate to any cell in the column. Then, I use Alt+O, C, W, (f<u>o</u>rmat, <u>c</u>olumn, and <u>w</u>idth). Then, I type 2 into the Column Width dialog box and press Enter.

Now that you have the Skinny Column set up, it is easy to insert a new column each month and ensure that the Totals automatically include the new column.

CHAPTER CONCLUSION

I think that pretty much wraps up the Skinny Row and Column Techniques. They have served me very well over the past 15 years, and I hope you can benefit from them as well.

Chapter 13: Hide Worksheets

I am not a big fan of hiding rows, columns, or sheets from the user. I believe that hiding stuff typically impedes maintenance and updates. However, there are times when hiding areas of a workbook from a user is a good thing. In this chapter, we'll discuss hiding worksheets. In a future book, we'll discuss the best way to hide columns or rows by using the Data Outline Group feature.

SET UP

If you recall, earlier in this series I tried to distinguish between a workbook administrator who initially develops the workbook, and a workbook user who maintains the workbook on an ongoing basis.

XREF

The difference between a workbook administrator and user is discussed in Chapter 3.

Sometimes, the workbook administrator may include notes, settings, assumptions, or other data that is not relevant to the user. In some cases, the productivity of the user may be increased when this extraneous information is hidden (that is, "out of sight, out of mind"). Efficiency may be improved in these cases, since the user won't be bogged down working with sheets that aren't relevant. Furthermore, the risk that the user will break the workbook is minimized.

It is often convenient to place your admin data on a worksheet, and then hide the worksheet so that it does not appear to a user.

> **NOTE**
>
> Please bear in mind that placing data on a hidden sheet doesn't truly prevent the user from gaining access to this data, since, depending on the security settings, a user may be able to unhide the sheet. So, the appropriate information to place on the hidden sheet includes notes or data that the user doesn't need, but which would be all right for a user to view if discovered. For example, sensitive payroll data should not be stored within a hidden sheet. See the XREFs below if you are interested in exploring additional built-in Excel security features.

Examples of admin information may include notes, change logs, tables, and assumptions: information that the user is unlikely to change, access, or need. Indeed, many of the workbooks that I develop include my internal notes on a hidden sheet. As I make changes to the workbook, I'll simply unhide my admin sheet, update my notes, and then hide the sheet once again before delivering it to the user. Thus, hiding a worksheet can be an effective way to manage workbooks, especially when the workbook administrator and the workbook user are different people.

HOW TO

It is actually quite easy to hide a worksheet. Of course, we are talking about Excel, so there are several ways to hide a sheet. One of the quickest ways to do this with a mouse is to right-click the sheet's tab and then select Hide. You can also use the Ribbon. First activate the sheet; for example, consider the sheet named Admin, which is the active sheet in Figure 52 below.

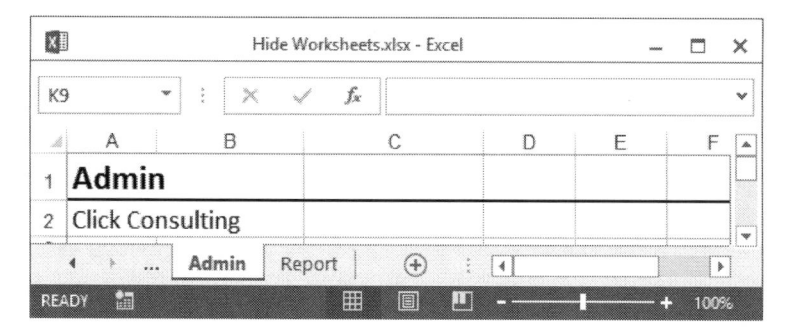

Figure 52

Once the sheet is active, navigate to the following command:

- RibbonUI: Home > Format > Hide & Unhide > Hide Sheet
- MenuUI: Format > Sheets > Hide

The hidden sheet is still in the workbook, however, its visibility is turned off so that it doesn't appear, and you can't navigate to it. You can see in Figure 53 below that the Admin sheet no longer appears as a tab since it is hidden.

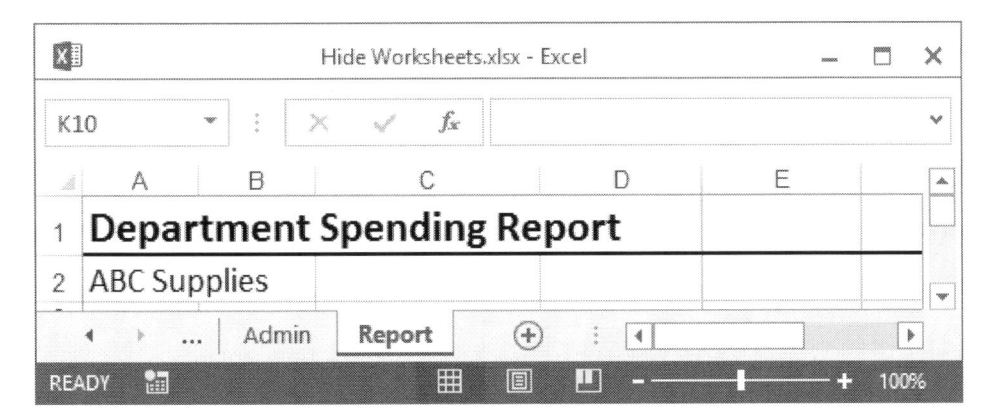

Figure 53

It is important to realize that formulas in any of the worksheets continue to have access to the cells and values on the sheet, even after it has been hidden, and, that is great, because we can store assumptions there and refer to them throughout the workbook.

KB

The keyboard sequence I use to hide a sheet is Alt+O, H, H (f<u>o</u>rmat, s<u>h</u>eet, <u>h</u>ide).

HOW TO UNHIDE

It is simple to unhide a sheet. Probably the quickest way is to right click any visible sheet's tab, and then select Unhide. You'll be presented with the Unhide dialog box, within which you can select the sheet to unhide.

You can also activate the Unhide dialog box by using the following command:

- RibbonUI: Home > Format > Hide & Unhide > Unhide Sheet
- MenuUI: Format > Sheets > Unhide

Select the sheet you would like to unhide and click OK. If all goes well, your sheet will appear once again.

KB

The keyboard sequence I use to unhide a sheet is Alt+O, H, U (f<u>o</u>rmat, <u>s</u>heet, <u>u</u>nhide).

XREF

The above discussion shows how to hide worksheets. Using the technique described, the hidden worksheets will appear in the Unhide dialog box. If you need to prevent a hidden sheet from appearing in the Unhide dialog box, you can make the sheet Very Hidden. This is explored in detail in a subsequent book in the macro discussion. However, if you can't wait, set the Visible property of the sheet to xlSheetVeryHidden in the visual basic editor.

XREF

Excel contains several built-in security features. When workbook protection is turned on, the user can't hide, unhide, delete, insert, or rename worksheets. A full discussion of workbook security is found in a subsequent book.

I know this is quite easy, but we'll still walk through an exercise workbook just so you can play with the process if you'd like.

EXAMPLES

We'll practice hiding worksheets by using an example.

PRACTICE

If you'd like to follow along, please refer to Hide Worksheets.xlsx.

VIDEO

To watch me complete the exercises, please visit the Excel University video library at www.clickconsulting.com/books.

In this example, you'll hide a worksheet that contains information designed for the workbook administrator.

PRACTICE

To follow along, please refer to the Exercise 1 worksheet.

Start by navigating to the worksheet that you'd like to hide. In this case, we'll use the "Admin" worksheet. Hide the sheet using any one of the techniques discussed above. For example, right click on the sheet tab and select Hide.

If all goes well, your Admin sheet will be hidden.

Please note that the company name on the Report sheet is a formula cell that obtains its value from the Admin sheet. Even though the Admin sheet is hidden, the formula still works. You can update the Company name value on the Admin sheet, and then hide the sheet. You'll notice that the Company name on the Report sheet has updated as well. This is exactly the desired behavior because it allows us to place various settings, assumptions, and other values on the Admin sheet and reference these values throughout the workbook.

NOTE

In the real world, I would have created a Name for the Company Name cell on the Admin sheet. Most likely, I would have named the cell co_name to indicate the company name. In this example however, I didn't set up the name because I wanted you to be able to see that the formula on the Report sheet contains a reference to the Admin sheet. Had I named the cell and used the name in the formula, it would have masked the fact that the source for the value is the Admin sheet.

CHAPTER CONCLUSION

That is my intro to hidden worksheets. We'll explore additional details and uses for this feature as we progress through this course.

Chapter 14: Highlight Input Cells

Surprisingly, highlighting input cells can increase the efficiency of maintaining your workbooks over time. This technique is especially important to incorporate into workbooks that you build for others to maintain.

SET UP

What does it mean to highlight an input cell? Well, there are really two parts to that question. First, what does it mean to highlight a cell? Second, what is an input cell, and how is it different from any other cell?

To highlight a cell is to apply some type of formatting to the cell to make it stand out. A simple example is to apply a yellow fill to the cell. An input cell is a cell that requires user input. A user does not need to worry about updating the values in any of the other cells in the worksheet. These other cells may contain formulas, text, or values or they may be empty. Highlighted input cells show the user which cells need attention. This technique helps the user efficiently perform updates.

Does taking the time to highlight input cells seem like a waste of time? You may spend more time up front highlighting, and thus it will take longer in the short term. But if the workbook is used recurrently, you'll quickly see how this technique saves time in the long run.

Can highlighting input cells improve efficiency? I haven't performed a formal study to answer this question, but based on my own first-hand observations, a user can update worksheets more quickly when input cells are highlighted. It has been my experience that this technique improves productivity for workbooks used on a recurring basis, say monthly, quarterly, or annually. In my work, I update the same set of workbooks each month. Even though I use the exact same set of workbooks repeatedly, each time I open one of those workbooks, it takes me a little while to remember how to update the workbook. It may take me some time to look through the cells and remember which ones I need to update. Plus, if I am rushing, I may accidentally enter a value into a formula cell, thereby introducing errors and inefficiencies into my workbook.

> **NOTE**
>
> Using worksheet protection, you can prevent a user from entering a value into selected cells, such as formula cells. You can even prevent the user from selecting or activating locked cells.

> **XREF**
>
> Worksheet protection is discussed at length in the security section in a subsequent book.

Identifying the cells that require a user's input will result in workbooks that are more efficient, because they will take less time to update. Also, these workbooks will generally be more accurate because formula cells are less likely to be overwritten by user input.

Applying a special format is a simple way to identify input cells. It really doesn't matter what kind of formatting you use, but you may want to be consistent with your department or company so that everyone is on the same page.

In the old days (Excel 2003 and earlier), I simply changed the font color to blue for input cells. This worked well for me for about a decade. Microsoft formally acknowledged the benefit of highlighting input cells with the release of Excel 2007 by including a cell style designed for this purpose. Indeed, Microsoft named the cell style Input, which is perfect. I now use this cell style to identify input cells.

HOW TO

One approach to highlighting an input cell is to apply cell formatting. For example, when you set up an input cell, you change the cell fill to yellow, and you can continue to manually apply cell formatting until the workbook is set up. For simple workbooks, this approach works just fine. However, this is not an efficient approach for more sophisticated workbooks, such as those with numerous input cells. You see, if you ever want to change the formatting you use to identify input cells, you'll need to go back through the workbook and manually change the formatting for each input cell. Thus, a better approach is to use a cell style. A style contains formatting information, such as fill color and border styles. You can apply a style to a cell instead of manually formatting a cell. You can change the style definition, and all of the cells with that style are immediately updated. Thus, I prefer to use styles to highlight input cells.

XREF

Beyond the built-in cell styles discussed here, you can build custom cell styles and modify the built-in cell styles. Styles are discussed in a subsequent book.

To apply a built-in style, start by selecting the input cell (or range of input cells), as shown in Figure 54 below.

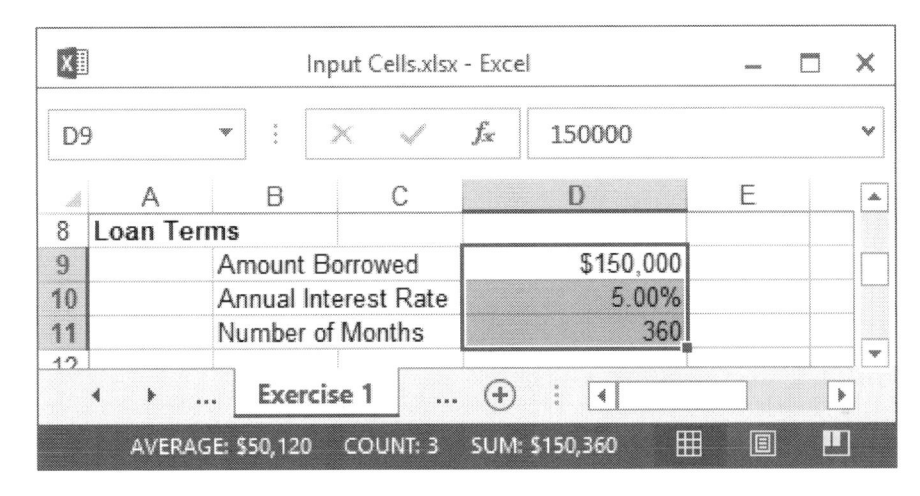

Figure 54

NOTE

You may be viewing the screenshot in black and white, so it may be hard to tell, but the cells above have no formatting (other than number formatting). They are highlighted because I selected the range.

Once the cells have been selected, apply the style by using the following command:

- RibbonUI: Home > Cell Styles > Input
- MenuUI: Format > Cell > Styles [Input style unavailable]

> **NOTE**
>
> Many new cell styles, including the Input style, were introduced beginning with Excel 2007. If you are following along with a previous version, please note that the Input cell style may not be available.

Microsoft defined the Input style format with peach cell fill and gray borders, as shown in Figure 55 below.

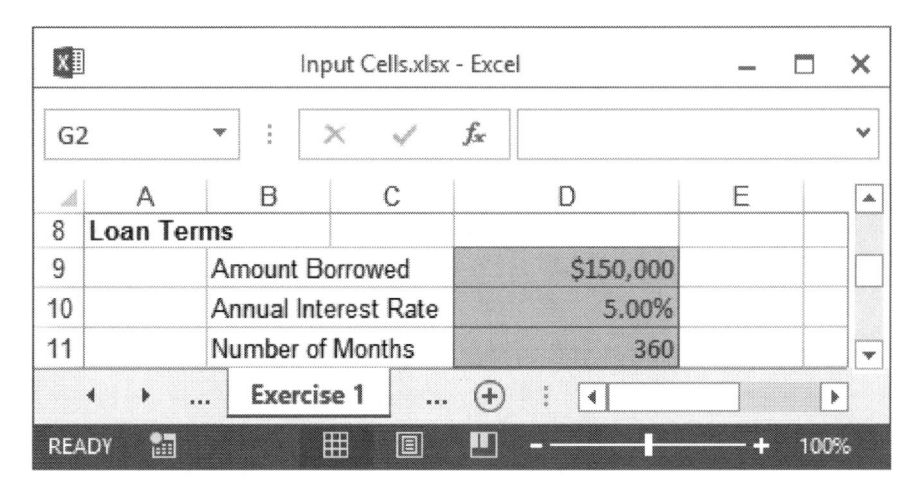

Figure 55

> **NOTE**
>
> You may be viewing the screenshot above in black and white, and thus it may be hard to tell, but the cells have a peach colored fill, with a gray cell border.

You can obviously select any other built-in style that suits your fancy. Throughout the remainder of this course, I'll be using the Input style.

Ready to play? Let's crack open the exercise workbook to get some practice.

EXAMPLES

In the following exercise workbook, you'll be highlighting input cells by using the built-in Input cell style.

🔘 PRACTICE

To follow along, please refer to the Input Cells.xlsx workbook.

▶ VIDEO

To watch me complete the exercises, please visit the Excel University video library at www.clickconsulting.com/books.

MONTHLY PAYMENT

In this exercise, you'll highlight the input cells in a worksheet that computes the monthly payment of a loan with specific terms. Other people in your company use this worksheet as a template, so you'd like it to be very clear and easy to use. Thus, you decide to identify the input cells so users can easily enter the loan assumptions.

🔘 PRACTICE

To follow along, please refer to the Exercise 1 worksheet.

Start by selecting the cells that represent the input cells. In this case, the input cells are the ones that store the amount borrowed, the annual interest rate, and the number of months.

After the input cells are selected, the next step is to apply the formatting. In this case, please use the built-in Input cell style so that we are consistent. In the real world though, please feel free to use any cell formatting or style that you prefer.

To apply the Input cell style, simply select the following command:

- RibbonUI: Home > Cell Styles > Input
- MenuUI: Feature unavailable

If all went well, those cells should now be formatted with a peach fill and a gray border.

🔄 XREF

The function used in this exercise worksheet to compute the monthly payment, PMT, will be discussed in detail later in a subsequent book.

JOURNAL ENTRY

For this exercise, pretend you are the primary user of this workbook. You use this Journal Entry workbook each month to help close the books. You'd like to highlight the input cells so you'll be able to update it more quickly and accurately each month.

PRACTICE

To follow along, please refer to the Exercise 2 worksheet.

Begin by selecting the input cells, which in this case are the cells for the date and the bank fees for each bank. Next, apply the built-in Input cell style to these cells. It will now be easy to see which cells need to be updated each month as you process your journal entry.

XREF

The function used in the exercise worksheet, EOMONTH, is discussed at length in a subsequent book.

REPORTING

For this exercise, pretend you deliver digital reports internally. You'd like to make it clear to your report users how they can update the report settings, so you decide to highlight the relevant input cells.

PRACTICE

To follow along, please refer to the Exercise 3 worksheet.

In this workbook, the user can change the report's Start Date and End Date. By updating those two values, the user can control which data flows into the report. Select these input cells and then apply the Input cell style.

XREF

The SUMIFS function used in this exercise worksheet is discussed at length in a subsequent book.

Now, look at the report worksheet. Consider what it looked like before highlighting the input cells. Cell formatting was uniform, thus making it difficult for the user to figure out that settings could be changed. Now, reflect on how much clearer it is for the user after you highlighted the input cells.

WITH DATA VALIDATION

For this exercise, let's say you want to deliver an interactive digital report. You'd like your report reader to be able to select a period. The formulas will provide the correct data for the period selected.

Your formulas were designed to process the specified month, provided the month is expressed as a three-letter abbreviation, such as Jan, Feb, or Mar. If the month is entered as a full month name, such as January or February, the formulas won't work. So, you have two tasks in this exercise; you need to highlight the input cell, and you need to use Data Validation to restrict the user's entry to valid month abbreviations.

PRACTICE

To follow along, please refer to the Exercise 4 worksheet.

XREF

Data Validation is discussed in Chapter 9.

First, you apply the Input style to the input cell. Then, you set up Data Validation on the input cell to make it easy for the user and to ensure that the selection provides the expected abbreviations to the formulas. As a result, it is easier for the user to identify the input cell and select a month from the drop down list. The Data Validation feature along with the identification of input cells through highlighting is a powerful way to improve efficiency.

CHAPTER CONCLUSION

I hope that this chapter has demonstrated the benefits of highlighting user input cells. We'll be highlighting input cells throughout the remainder of the workbooks used in this course.

Chapter 15: Workbook Organization

Did you know that you could gain efficiency just by the way you organize the worksheets within your workbooks? Productivity is likewise improved when you properly organize the data within your worksheets. This chapter discusses workbook organization concepts, while the next chapter discusses worksheet organization concepts.

DEPENDS ON

Content is this chapter assumes you know how to highlight input cells, Chapter 14 and hide worksheets, Chapter 13.

SET UP

As you can already tell, I am just a little obsessed with efficiency. Doing things in just a fraction of the time it takes others makes me happy. This desire to maximize efficiency has caused me to analyze productivity in virtually every area of Excel, including how I organize worksheets within a workbook.

This chapter discusses the techniques that I use to organize my workbooks. It is my hope that these concepts can help improve your productivity as you continue your exploration of the greatest software application of all time, Microsoft Excel.

HOW TO

There are a handful of workbook organization concepts, and we'll work through them one by one. After we discuss the concepts, we'll use an exercise workbook to practice. Specifically, we'll explore the following concepts:

- Name All Sheets
- No Extra Sheets
- Start Here
- ErrorCk
- Admin
- Match Data Flow
- Color Code
- Print Order
- Index

NAME ALL SHEETS

First, it is important to assign a meaningful name to each worksheet. The default sheet names (Sheet1, Sheet2, and Sheet3) offer no indication of the content, causing users to waste time navigating through each sheet to find the information they need.

It is easy to change the name of a worksheet, and there are many ways to accomplish this. You can right-click the sheet tab and select Rename, double-click on the sheet tab, or select the sheet and then click the following command:

- RibbonUI: Home > Format > Rename Sheet
- MenuUI: Format > Sheets > Rename

Be sure to provide a short but meaningful name.

KB

The keyboard sequence I use to rename a sheet is Alt+O, H, R (f<u>o</u>rmat, s<u>h</u>eet, <u>r</u>ename).

NO EXTRA SHEETS

Another perpetual time waster is to have extra blank sheets in a workbook. Generally, a user feels compelled to cycle through and look at all of the sheets in a workbook during a review. Thus, I recommend removing all blank sheets from workbooks.

It is easy to delete an unused worksheet. You can right-click on the sheet tab and then select Delete or you can use the following command:

- RibbonUI: Home > Delete > Delete Sheet
- MenuUI: Edit > Delete Sheet

XREF

You can group select many sheets and then delete them all at the same time. For more information, please visit the Sheet Selection Groups discussion in Chapter 18.

KB

The keyboard shortcut I use to delete the active sheet: Alt+E, L (edit, delete). To insert a new sheet, I use Alt+I, W (insert, worksheet).

Did you know that you could change the number of blank sheets that are included in new workbooks? By changing this value to something small, such as one, you won't have to spend time removing extra blank sheets. Simply select the following command:

- RibbonUI: File > Options > General
- MenuUI: Tools > Options > General

Then, change the Include This Many Sheets value down to something small, like 1.

START HERE

In most of the workbooks I develop, the first sheet is called Start Here. This worksheet plays an important part in workbook organization.

Think of the Start Here sheet as the sheet that users will naturally navigate to when they first crack open the workbook. It should contain basic settings, maintenance instructions, assumptions, and other general information.

In most of my Start Here sheets, I typically include the following areas:

Title

The worksheet Title, for example, Start Here.

Company

The company name, such as Click Consulting.

Purpose

The purpose of the workbook is stated high up on the sheet. For example, "The purpose of this workbook is to obtain QuickBooks export data and convert it into a summary SG&A report by department."

Settings

These settings refer to user-entered settings and input cells. For example, you may ask your user to enter a Company Name, Closing Period, Start Date, End Date, Department, User Name, and so on. The values entered here are typically used by formulas and functions elsewhere in the workbook. It is a great idea to name each input cell with a meaningful name so that it is easy to use the value throughout your workbook. Remember to highlight the input cells!

> **XREF**
>
> Input cell highlighting is discussed in Chapter 14.

> **XREF**
>
> Named references are discussed in Chapter 7.

INSTRUCTIONS

This area of the Start Here sheet should include instructions to the user on how to maintain the workbook over time. For example, "To update this workbook each month, open QuickBooks and export the memorized report named 'SGA data', paste the data into the QBData worksheet, and then view the updated report on the Report sheet." If your workbook has some sophisticated formulas or functions, it may be helpful to explain their purpose, logic, and arguments. Instructions for how to update and how to maintain the workbook over time are essential to maximizing productivity and efficiency.

Assumptions

Any assumptions you made as you built the workbook should be well documented. If you built the formulas based on the assumption that the Region will be in column A, then you should document this. If the user enters the Region in column B, then your formulas will no longer work, and the workbook will break. The user should be able to review the assumptions to ensure that data was entered properly, and if not, be able to identify how to correct it. Think of this area as your "disclaimer" area, where you tell the user that the workbook may break under certain conditions and when certain assumptions are not satisfied. For example, "The workbook assumes that the data from QuickBooks maintains the same column order over time, namely, that Name is in column C and Amount is in column F." Another example is "The Data sheet must be sorted in ascending order." Include references to formulas and specific cells or worksheets as necessary. If something goes awry, the user's first task would be to check out the assumptions to be sure they are met.

Support

At the bottom of the Start Here sheet you should include a note about whom to contact if support on the workbook is needed. For example, "For support, please contact Jeff Lenning of Click Consulting at clickconsulting.com." Be sure to include your extension, email address, or other contact information. Perhaps the support area doesn't list an individual person; maybe it is a specific department within your company, such as Finance or Accounting. You get the idea.

Feel free to use a different name than Start Here if you prefer. Perhaps a name like Settings, Assumptions, or Instructions would work best. Just be sure to include this basic information in your workbooks. You'll find that as the workbook lives on, it will be more efficient to maintain. That means increased productivity for you and your company.

ERRORCK

The second worksheet you'll find in most of my workbooks is a sheet named ErrorCk. This is a key worksheet because it improves accuracy and promotes efficiency.

The purpose of the ErrorCk worksheet is to monitor conditions throughout the workbook. For example, you may want to monitor the balance sheet to ensure assets equal liabilities and equity. When a condition is not met, such as the balance sheet is out of balance, the ErrorCk will display an alert. On this single worksheet, you can verify that all conditions have been met and that all tests have passed. This sheet gives you the confidence to rely on Excel as you delegate more work to Excel.

Delegating work to Excel means less manual entry, which means that you feel less familiar with the numbers in the workbook. In the old days, you may have hand-keyed data and you probably reviewed the numbers while you entered them. If you delegate more of your work to Excel, then your workbooks will require less data entry. Thus, it is a good idea to have Excel assist with your review process. The ErrorCk sheet becomes one of the steps in your review. It is a control point that helps ensure that the data is flowing properly throughout the workbook and that the numbers tie.

There are many tests or conditions that we can monitor. For example, we could set up a test to verify that debits equal credits. We could verify that assets equal liabilities and equity; that the cash balance on the balance sheet agrees to the cash balance on the cash flow statement; that net income per the income statement ties to the cash flow statement, and that the trial balance foots to zero.

In workbooks that are more sophisticated, we'll want a way to ensure that the data flows from one sheet to another as expected. For example, let's say that we export data from QuickBooks and paste it in to a sheet named QBData. We have a worksheet that uses sophisticated formulas to aggregate the values in the QBData sheet into a summary report. We need to ensure that all data on the QBData sheet made it into to the Report sheet. This test is performed on the ErrorCk worksheet by comparing the total on the QBData sheet to the total on the Report sheet. If these totals do not agree, we know there is an issue; for example, maybe a new account was added to QuickBooks, and our report needs to be updated to include this new account. The ErrorCk alerts us and provides a quick way to review.

It is probably best to build the ErrorCk tests as you build the workbook. While you are building the various worksheets in the workbook and you notice a condition that would indicate an error, be sure to set up a test on the ErrorCk.

Conditional formatting is a wonderful feature to use with ErrorCk worksheets. As you can imagine, you'll have many tests on the ErrorCk worksheet. Conditional formatting can draw your attention to failed tests with a bright red cell fill. I use conditional formatting in virtually all of my ErrorCk worksheets.

XREF

Conditional formatting is discussed in Chapter 10.

As we progress through this course, we'll explore the specific formulas and functions needed to set up a good ErrorCk sheet; for now, I just wanted to be sure to discuss this process conceptually.

> **XREF**
>
> One worksheet function that is useful when comparing cell values, for example on an ErrorCk worksheet, is the IF function, which is discussed in a subsequent book.

ADMIN

Sometimes I'll include an Admin worksheet in a workbook on which I'll store instructions or settings that the user won't need to be concerned with or modify. I'll also keep a log of the changes and enhancements that I've made over time. Since the user doesn't need to view it, I'll simply hide the Admin worksheet.

> **XREF**
>
> Hidden worksheets are discussed in Chapter 13.

When appropriate, feel free to include a hidden admin worksheet for your notes and assumptions as well. It can be quite handy at times.

MATCH DATA FLOW

It helps to arrange worksheets in a logical order. I like to line them up in the order of how a process flows. For example, my first two sheets are Start Here and ErrorCk. After that, I typically have additional input sheets and data sheets to store data imported from other accounting systems or applications. Next are any sheets that help process or remap that data. The last series of sheets are the report or output sheets that produce the intended results or achieve the workbook's stated purpose.

I have worked with others who feel more comfortable placing the report sheets toward the left, which is absolutely fine. Just be sure to organize your sheets in a logical order so that it is easy for the user to navigate through the workbook. It is probably best if your firm or company agrees to a standard so that workbooks are organized consistently across your company or firm.

COLOR CODE

Ever since 1996 or 1997, I've wished for a 3-D sheet interface, rather than the current 2-D sheet interface. A 3-D structure would provide an additional level of worksheet organization.

Excel currently lists worksheets as little tabs sequentially from left to right at the bottom of the Excel window. It would be wonderful if we could organize them in folders or somehow stack them in groups to help keep organized. For example, all of the Input sheets could go into the Input folder, or all of the report sheets could go into a reports folder. However, that feature does not exist to my knowledge.

But we can color code the sheet tabs. To be clear, I'm not talking about coloring the worksheet cells; rather, I'm talking about coloring the sheet's tab located at the bottom of the Excel window. For example, all of the Report sheet tabs can be blue, the input sheet tabs can be yellow, and the sheets that take data from QuickBooks can be green. This is one way to help organize worksheets and create groups or classes of sheets.

You can come up with any coloring scheme that you'd like. Typically, I'll use a peach tab for all input sheets, and those are typically the first set of sheets after Start Here and ErrorCk. I'll also use a green tab color to identify sheets that are simply imported from QuickBooks or other accounting systems. I'll use blue tabs for report sheets, and red for my ErrorCk sheet.

PRINT ORDER

When you deliver your Excel sheets as a report printed to paper or to PDF, be sure to organize the sheets within your workbook in the report Page order. This comes in handy when you group sheets and print them or when you work with macros, since they will print out in the same order in which they appear within the workbook.

INDEX

Have you ever worked in a workbook with few sheets, say three or four sheets? Navigating to the correct sheet is fast and easy, and you spend very little time getting to the spot you need to be to do your work.

Have you ever worked in a workbook with more sheets? Say, 10, 20, 100, or even 200 sheets? In these types of large workbooks, it takes a long time to get to the right sheet, doesn't it? To be clear, you waste time just trying to get to the right spot so that you can then begin your work.

In large workbooks, it may be useful to have a worksheet up front named Index or something similar. The index sheet simply has a hyperlink to each sheet in the workbook, and each sheet has a link back to the Index. This means that any sheet is only two clicks away. This technique can dramatically speed up your work, making you more productive, since you spend more of your time working and less of your time just getting to where you need to be before you can start your work. If you have never played with the hyperlink feature in Excel, don't worry, you will have done so by the time you are finished with this course!

XREF

We'll discuss Hyperlinks in detail in a subsequent book.

EXAMPLE

I'll now illustrate some of the above concepts with a workbook example.

PRACTICE

To follow along, please refer to Workbook Organization.xlsx.

NOTE

There are no hands-on exercises for this chapter. The sample workbook is provided to illustrate the concepts. There is not an answers version of the practice workbook.

At first glance, you'll notice that I've color-coded the sheet tabs. In the real world, I probably wouldn't color code tabs in such a small workbook (only four sheets), but, as the number of sheets grows, it becomes increasingly important to color code the sheet tabs. I use red for my error-checking sheet, green for incoming data, and blue for reports.

You'll also notice that each sheet is named, and that there are no blank or unused sheets.

Now, let's take a tour of the workbook, sheet by sheet.

START HERE WORKSHEET

Let's begin our tour with the first sheet in the book, the Start Here worksheet.

PRACTICE

If you are following along, please refer to the Start Here worksheet.

I first want to highlight a few things on this sheet. You'll notice the sheet name and company name are at the top, followed by the Purpose section. I guess this is a habit from my AA & Co. days, but I find that placing a Purpose statement on top of a worksheet helps to clarify the function of the sheet for users.

Next, you'll notice that the worksheet has a Settings section where the user can input values. You'll also notice that I highlighted the input cells using the built-in Input cell style, as shown in Figure 56 below.

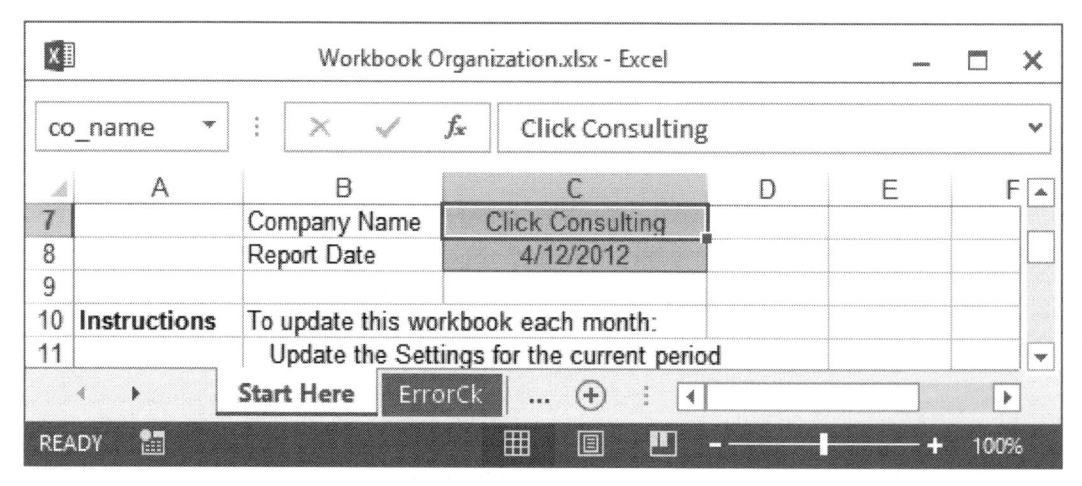

Figure 56

XREF

Using cell styles to highlight input cells is discussed in Chapter 14.

You'll notice that I included an input cell for the Company Name setting. This provides several benefits. If you are in public accounting or consulting, you'll quickly realize that you may be able to use this workbook for another client and easily change the client name throughout the workbook by updating the value in the input cell. If you are in industry, it is convenient to provide a Company Name input cell, not because you'll be changing your company name frequently, but because your company name is probably used on many sheets. Rather than typing the company name many times throughout the workbook, you can simply reference the input cell. Let's see how.

If you select the Company Name input cell, you'll notice by examining the Name Box (the box to the left of the formula bar) that I set up a name for the cell. Specifically, I named it co_name. Then, looking through the various sheets, you'll notice that in cells where I needed the company name, I used a simple formula to pull in the company name from the Start Here sheet:

```
=co_name
```

Centrally storing values that are used throughout a workbook is generally a good idea, and the Start Here sheet is a perfect spot to place all of these types of values.

The next input cell is the Report Date. Again, I provided a name so that I could easily refer to it throughout the workbook.

It is a good idea to name all of the input cells. This makes it easy to incorporate those values into cells, formulas, and functions. Later in this course we'll discuss the CONCATENATE function, which provides powerful ways to incorporate these values into our worksheets. Additionally, naming the input cells makes them easier to use in macros, which we'll discuss later in this course.

XREF

Named References are discussed in Chapter 7.

XREF

The CONCATENATE function is discussed in a subsequent book.

XREF

Macros are discussed in a subsequent book.

Next on the Start Here sheet is the Instructions section, which tells the user how to update the workbook each period. The people who maintain a workbook may change over time, and it's therefore important to ensure a process by which the workbook lives on and continues to provide accurate information. This is accomplished by creating instructions to future users, and the best time to write the instructions is when you first build the workbook.

The Assumptions section is next; here you can disclose the conditions under which the workbook will work. In other words, the workbook will operate properly when all of the assumptions are met. This information is critical with helping to ensure that the workbook continues to perform as expected.

The final section is called Support and tells users whom to contact if they are stuck or have questions.

ERRORCK WORKSHEET

The next worksheet in the workbook is the ErrorCk sheet.

> **PRACTICE**
>
> If you are following along, please refer to the ErrorCk worksheet.

You'll notice that I established several tests on the ErrorCk worksheet. One test, as shown in Figure 57 below, verifies that the data on the QBData sheet flowed into the Report sheet.

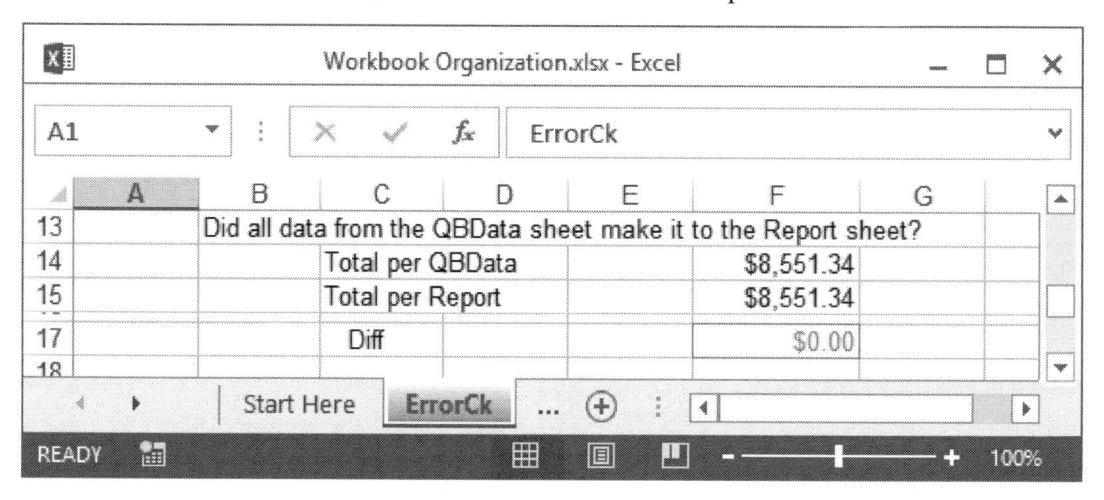

Figure 57

In an upcoming book in this course, we'll discuss how to use Boolean values and logic functions to improve the ErrorCk worksheet.

> **XREF**
>
> Boolean values and logic functions are discussed in a subsequent book.

As you can see on the ErrorCk sheet, I generally like to phrase my tests with yes/no questions so that the purpose of each test is clear. For example, "Did all data from the QBData sheet make it to the Report sheet?" as shown in cell B13, Figure 57 above. Next, I like to retrieve the required values from the various sheets using formulas as shown in cells F14 and F15 above. Last, I conditionally format the result and typically use a green cell border and font color when the data passes the test. I'll use red cell fill with white bold font to indicate that the data failed the test. Formatting the results makes it quicker to spot errors, since you won't need to spend time trying to read each test and test result.

XREF

Conditional formatting is discussed in Chapter 10.

Remember that this is your key control sheet, and with it you can quickly gain comfort that the mechanics within the workbook are accurate. In the real world, you'll set up as many tests as needed to look for various errors. You want to try to anticipate errors and ways in which future users could break the workbook.

XREF

The YEAR function used in the sample workbook is discussed in a subsequent book.

QBDATA WORKSHEET

The QBData sheet is a place for the user to paste in the QuickBooks accounting data.

PRACTICE

If you are following along, please refer to the QBData worksheet.

If you don't use QuickBooks, then just imagine that this sheet represents incoming data from whatever accounting system you use.

Notice that I used a Table to store the data, as shown in Figure 58 below. Tables automatically expand as new data is added, eliminating the need to update formulas on the Report sheet in subsequent periods.

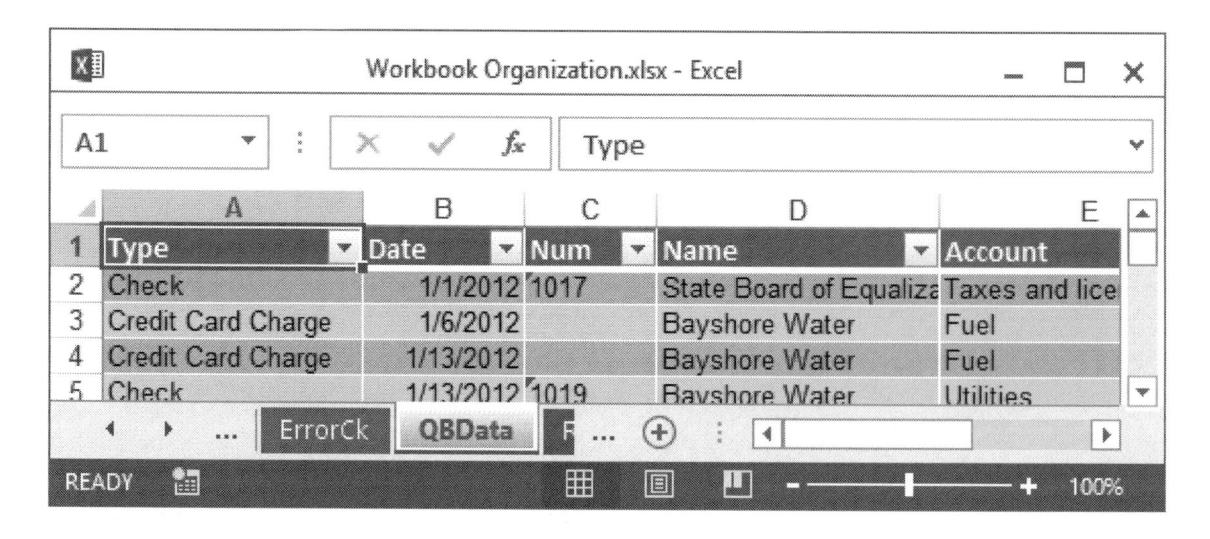

Figure 58

XREF

Tables are discussed in Chapter 8.

A NOTE ABOUT IMPORTING DATA

I'd like to highlight three typical methods for getting data from a system, such as an accounting system, into Excel:

- Copy/Paste
- Pull
- Push

In the Copy/Paste method, you export the data from an accounting system to a new Excel, csv, or text file, and then copy the data and paste it into the destination sheet. This approach often works well with many accounting systems and is simple to use. However the other methods may be more efficient for recurring processes.

In the Pull method, we tell Excel to go to the external system and retrieve specified data. This method uses an Excel feature called External Data, which we'll discuss at length in the future, but if you want to experiment now, please feel free. Once the data definition has been established, updating the data region in subsequent periods is accomplished by clicking a Refresh button. Thus, retrieving data from external systems on a recurring basis can be quite efficient when using the Pull method, which works with many accounting systems, but not all.

In the Push method, we instruct the accounting system to export data directly into a specific worksheet within a specific Excel workbook, which eliminates the need to subsequently copy and paste the data to the correct sheet. Not all accounting systems support this method. Using QuickBooks as an example, you can export a report or transaction listing into an existing workbook, and, within this workbook to a specific worksheet. When this approach is used, take care to set up formulas that will continue to work even if more data is exported in subsequent periods, such as by using column-only references. We'll explore this method in complete detail in the future.

XREF

The External Data feature is discussed in a subsequent book.

XREF

Working with QuickBooks is discussed in a subsequent book.

REPORT WORKSHEET

The last worksheet in this workbook is the report sheet.

PRACTICE

If you are following along, please refer to the Report worksheet.

The report sheet simply contains formulas that compute the report summary and report detail sections, essentially summarizing the data from the QBData sheet. The summary section of the report is shown in Figure 59 below.

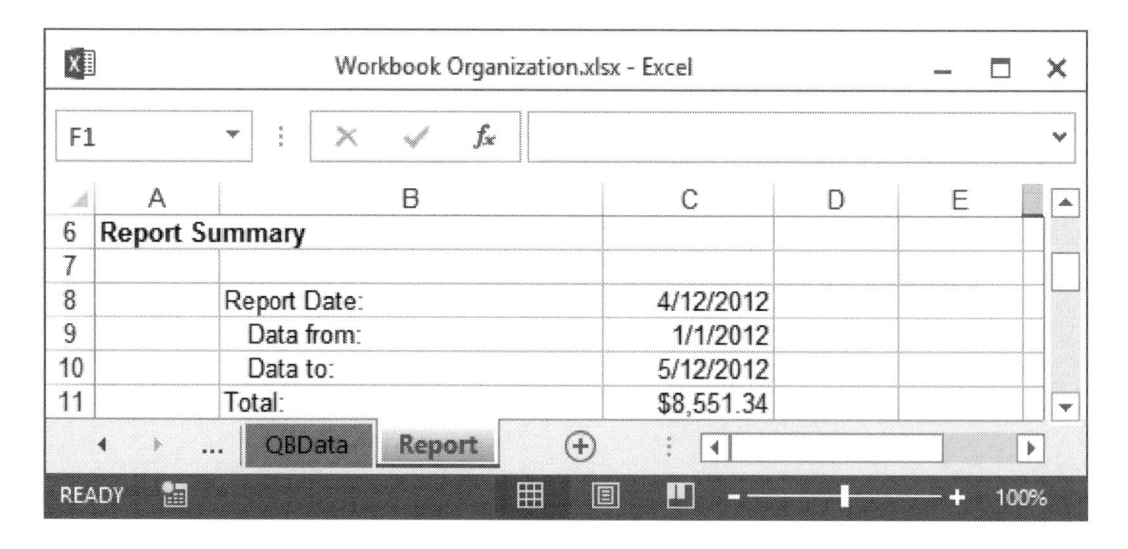

Figure 59

This report is hands-off. What I mean is that since the report is formula based, there is no need to manually type values into any cells or enter anything on the report sheet. The formulas instantly compute the updated report results once the new data arrives into the workbook. It is generally a good habit to think about splitting data sheets from report sheets, so that the report sheets are entirely formula based. This concept allows you to create hands-off reports that are fully automatic. I'll be reinforcing this concept throughout the entire series.

CHAPTER CONCLUSION

I hope that the tips discussed in this chapter will provide value to you as you work in Excel.

Chapter 16: Worksheet Organization

SET UP

Setting up workbooks the right way helps to automate recurring processes and minimize the manual steps involved. The automation of recurrent workbooks is a theme examined throughout this series, and it is fairly obvious that the exploration of Excel features and functions is a critical part of our discussion. However, what may not be as obvious is the fact that automation begins even before we select the functions and features. It starts with the way we structure the workbook and even more specifically, the data within each worksheet.

I'm often called to consult on various Excel workbooks and projects, and in many cases the client's challenges are simply due to poor worksheet design. By not considering the worksheet and data flow, and haphazardly placing data into the worksheet, the client has to spend time on overly complex formulas and maintenance. Had the data been placed into the worksheet correctly, the formulas would be easier and the labor required for maintenance would be less. Being intentional about the way we configure our worksheets and organize data can make a big difference. This chapter is designed to walk through several worksheet design ideas.

HOW TO

When building a workbook, it is important to carefully consider how you design the data sheets and report structure. You'll want to structure them in a way that will allow you to use simple functions and minimize the amount of manual steps involved, especially when the workbook is used on an ongoing or recurring basis.

Sometimes you have almost no control over the format of the data or report structure. Data format restrictions may be imposed by the accounting system exports, and you pretty much have to deal with the data as it comes. Report structure restrictions may be imposed by your client, boss, or whoever requires a very specific and precise report layout. When there are such restrictions, we do our best to automate our tasks but realize that these constraints may cause us to implement overly sophisticated formulas and functions or necessitate the use of macros. Oftentimes, however, we do have some control over the incoming data format and report structure. In these cases we can simplify our formulas and improve productivity.

Assume for a moment that we import some data from an accounting system and place this imported data into a worksheet. Next, assume that we use this imported data as the basis for a report located on another worksheet. The export format may not be optimal for building our report, but by adjusting the export format, we may simplify our tasks in Excel. Perhaps we can change the export to include needed columns, exclude unnecessary columns, remove subtotals, or flatten the export from a multicolumn hierarchy.

To illustrate this idea, consider an export that places amounts in 12 monthly columns, such as Jan, Feb, Mar, and so on. For this particular report, we could simplify our formulas by transposing the data's structure to a single Amount column plus a Date column. By changing the orientation of the data from amounts placed horizontally in 12 columns to amounts stacked vertically in a single column, we are able to use the SUMIFS function instead of more sophisticated, and perhaps nested, lookup functions. Plus, we could easily compute a year-to-date total or sum values within a specific date range since the SUMIFS function supports the use of comparison operators. In other words, the report we need to generate becomes much easier for us if we can use the SUMIFS function, and we can easily use the SUMIFS function if the data comes to us vertically. Therefore, before using an approach that requires more sophisticated formulas, you should find out if the export format could be modified, especially for recurring reports.

XREF

The SUMIFS is discussed in a subsequent book.

NOTE

In some cases, we may encounter a limitation of our accounting system. It may not be able to export data in a format optimal for use with Excel, but we may be able to bypass this limitation by using Microsoft Access as an intermediate step because we have full control over the query definitions and data structure as it flows into Excel. Microsoft Access is discussed in a subsequent book.

In terms of the report, we can often adjust the structure in a way that does not affect the report user or the value of the report, but does simplify the formulas and functions being used. For example, rather than nesting Quarter subtotals within the monthly columns (e.g., Jan, Feb, Mar, Qtr1, Apr, May, Jun, Qtr2, etc.), we place the Quarter subtotals outside and after the monthly columns (Jan, Feb…Dec, Qtr1, Qtr2, Qtr3, Qtr4). This slight adjustment probably won't affect the report user, but it will greatly improve the speed with which the workbook is maintained and updated.

So, as you can imagine, the structure we use for data and reports matters. Structuring worksheets the right way absolutely improves our productivity. Let's discuss several specific worksheet design concepts, including:

- Split Data from Report Sheets
- Flat Data
- Clean Data
- Uniform Data
- Accommodate Minor Structure Changes
- As It Comes
- Subtotals Outside
- Subtotals Above
- Consistent Formulas in a Region
- Sheet Title
- Company Name
- Column A for Labels; Begin Data in Column B
- Sheet Names Short but Descriptive
- Prefer Lookups to Direct Cell References
- No Blank Columns
- Consistent Headers

SPLIT DATA FROM REPORT SHEETS

Generally it is a good idea to split the data from the report. That is, to place the data on one sheet and the report on a different sheet. Sometimes there are restrictions, and the report and data must be on the same sheet. However, when the report is a summary or aggregation of the data, it is best to place the data on one sheet and the report on another. This helps to automate recurring processes, because each month you simply paste the new data on the data sheet, and then the report sheet's smart formulas automatically summarize the values. The report is hands-off because it is automatically updated when new data arrives in the data worksheet.

FLAT DATA

Excel is best equipped to summarize data that is in a flat format. Data can come from a variety of sources, such as being manually keyed in, but the most common source is from another program or application. Whenever possible, it is best to get the data in a flat format.

A flat format means that there is one row for each record, and there is no structural relationship or hierarchy to the data. In other words, each row contains all values for the record, with no information about the record coming from other rows or the record's position in the list. Flat data often repeats values, for example, consider the Name column shown in Figure 60 below.

	B	C	D	E
8	**Name**	**Account**	**Date**	**Amount**
9	Bayshore Water	Fuel	4/28/2012	24.00
10	Bayshore Water	Fuel	5/5/2012	24.50
11	Bayshore Water	Fuel	5/12/2012	25.00
12	Bayshore Water	Utilities	5/12/2012	38.75
13	Cal Gas & Electric	Office expenses	1/21/2012	156.22
14	Cal Gas & Electric	Office expenses	2/25/2012	122.51
15	Cal Gas & Electric	Office expenses	3/24/2012	113.89
16	Cal Gas & Electric	Office expenses	4/21/2012	118.50
17	CalOil Company	Rent of other business	2/10/2012	66.56
18	CalOil Company	Rent of other business	3/17/2012	52.48

Figure 60

As you can see, there is one row for each record, and even though there are several transactions for Bayshore Water, the vendor name is repeated on each row. Thus, there is no structural relationship between the records; each row provides all necessary information for the record without requiring any information from other rows. The worksheet could be resorted in any order, and the data would still make sense. This is an ideal format for use with Excel. This format allows us to use many cool features and functions, including PivotTables, AutoFilter, sorting, subtotals, and SUMIFS. We would be precluded from using these features if the data were not flat.

Some accounting applications export data in a format that is not flat, and this forces us to use overly complex formulas, restricts our use of features, and may necessitate the use of macros. Consider the export shown in Figure 61 below.

Name	Account	Date	Amount
Bayshore Water	Fuel	4/28/2012	24.00
		5/5/2012	24.50
		5/12/2012	25.00
	Utilities	5/12/2012	38.75
Cal Gas & Electric	Office expenses	1/21/2012	156.22
		2/25/2012	122.51
		3/24/2012	113.89
		4/21/2012	118.50
CalOil Company	Rent of other business	2/10/2012	66.56
		3/17/2012	52.48

Figure 61

This data format is not flat. Values for certain records are defined by the structure and order of the rows. I know that the transaction in row 39 is for Bayshore Water because the vendor name appears in column B. The only reason I know that the transaction in row 40 is for Bayshore Water is because it follows row 39. The vendor name of Bayshore Water does not appear in column B. If the worksheet were resorted, we would lose track of which transactions go with which vendors. Since not all needed data is self-contained within each row, this format is much more difficult to work with and limits our ability to use Excel's full capabilities. To use many of Excel's powerful features and functions, we would first need to spend time flattening the data, perhaps by running a macro. When we have control over the format, we should ensure the data is in a structure that allows us to easily use Excel's powerful features and functions.

CLEAN DATA

Whenever possible, try to use exported data that is clean. Clean data only includes a single column header label along with the raw table data. This means no print or page headers or footers, no subtotals embedded throughout the data, and no blank rows or columns. A nice, tight data region full of values is best for us, because this type of clean data is easy to use and enables us to take advantage of all of Excel's advanced features and functions.

When the data is not clean, we first need to spend time cleaning it up before we can begin our real work. If we need to do this on a recurring basis, we should explore the possibility of using a macro to format and clean the data region.

> **XREF**
>
> Macros are discussed is a subsequent book.

UNIFORM DATA

When setting up various worksheets in a workbook, you'll likely have some sheets that store data and some that store reports. It is best if these data and report sheets have a uniform structure and orientation. When the data layout is similar to the report layout, the formulas will be simplified, and thus ongoing maintenance will be easier.

For example, if all of the sheets, including data sheets and report sheets, are laid out in monthly columns, it is relatively easy to build the formulas because the data has the same orientation as the report.

However, if the report requires monthly columns, but the data sheet has a vertical orientation with monthly totals placed down in rows, your work will require overly complex formulas, since you'll need to transpose the data.

Therefore, whenever possible, keep the orientation and layout uniform and consistent between all worksheets in the workbook.

ACCOMMODATE MINOR STRUCTURE CHANGES

It is a good idea to anticipate minor structure changes that may occur over time and set up the worksheet to accommodate these slight changes.

For example, users may add new rows of data or need new subtotals during the course of their work. We previously discussed how to address both of these examples mechanically. Do you remember? Set up a Table so that as new data rows are added, formulas automatically include the new data. If you don't use a Table, use a Skinny Row. Use the SUBTOTAL function so that you can easily add new subtotal rows.

XREF

The SUBTOTAL function is discussed in Chapter 11.

XREF

Tables are discussed in Chapter 8.

XREF

Skinny Row is discussed in Chapter 12.

AS IT COMES

When our work begins with data originating from other data sources, we want to be sure to use formulas that operate on that data as it comes. That is, when we import data from another data source, we should seek to write formulas that operate on the data in the imported format so that we don't need to spend time manually changing the format. When this is not practical, consider the use of a macro to perform the reformatting.

SUBTOTALS OUTSIDE

When possible, try to place formula cells outside of data regions. Quarter subtotals are often embedded within the data, like this:

Jan	Feb	Mar	**Qtr1**	Apr	May	Jun	**Qtr2**	Jul	Aug	Sep	**Qtr3**	Oct	Nov	Dec	**Qtr4**

However, you want to place them outside of the data region, like this:

Jan	Feb	Mar	Apr	May	Jun	Jul	Aug	Sep	Oct	Nov	Dec	**Qtr1**	**Qtr2**	**Qtr3**	**Qtr4**

By keeping formulas outside of data regions, the worksheet will be easier to maintain over time.

SUBTOTALS ABOVE

Consider placing total formulas above the data when the number of rows of incoming data is always changing and you need to show a total, but you can't split the data sheet from the report sheet. Then, you won't need to insert rows or move your subtotal functions, you can simply paste in the new data under the formulas.

CONSISTENT FORMULAS IN A REGION

Try to make your formulas consistent within an area or region of the worksheet. This will make the formulas easy to maintain over time. When it is necessary, update the formula in the upper left cell of the range, and then fill it down and to the right.

Creating consistent formulas in a range is sometimes as easy as using the proper cell reference (absolute, relative, mixed). However, sometimes it requires a more sophisticated formula or the use of advanced lookup functions like CHOOSE and MATCH.

> **XREF**
>
> The CHOOSE function is discussed in a subsequent book.

> **XREF**
>
> The MATCH function is discussed in a subsequent book.

But I've discovered that for recurring workbooks, it's worth it to take the time to develop formulas that are consistent within a region.

SHEET TITLE

On the worksheet itself, probably up near cell A1, be sure to include the report name or sheet title. This will help users feel organized.

COMPANY NAME

Be sure each sheet includes the company name when applicable.

COLUMN A FOR LABELS; BEGIN DATA IN COLUMN B

Keep column A for sheet section labels, such as Purpose, Settings, Instructions, Report, Data, and so on. Begin the actual data in column B, as illustrated in Figure 62 below.

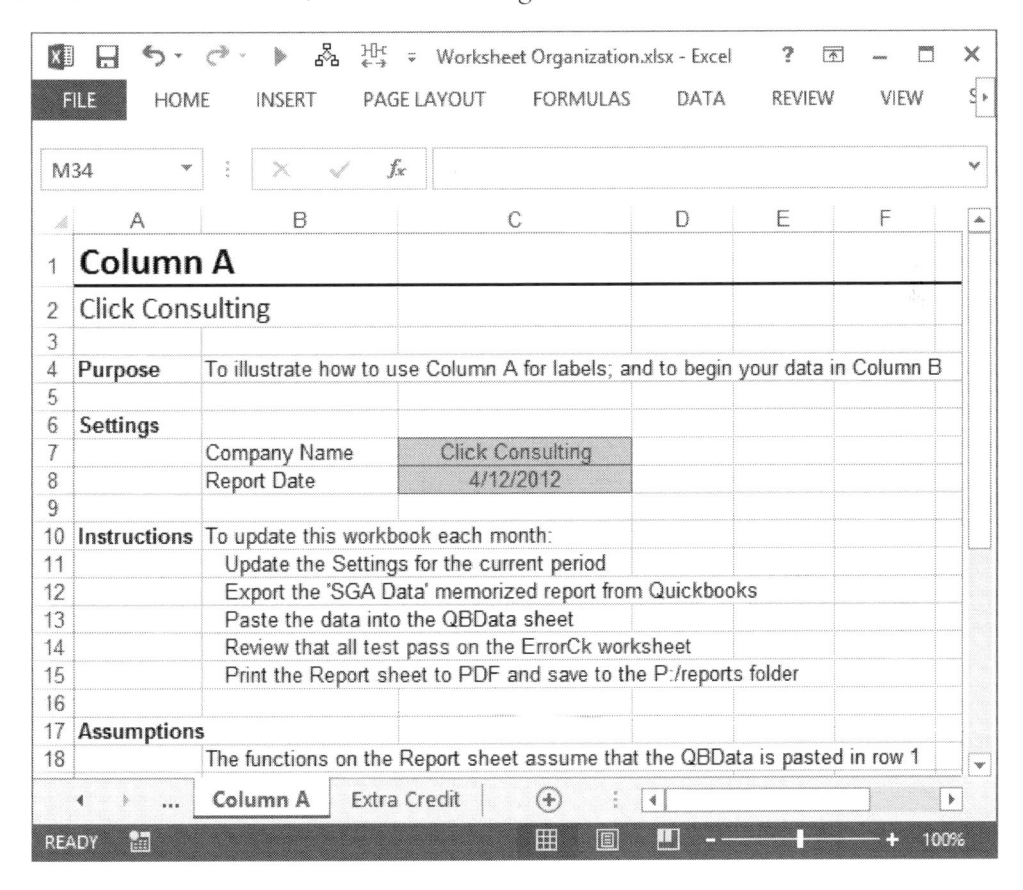

	A	B
1	Column A	
2	Click Consulting	
3		
4	Purpose	To illustrate how to use Column A for labels; and to begin your data in Column B
5		
6	Settings	
7		Company Name — Click Consulting
8		Report Date — 4/12/2012
9		
10	Instructions	To update this workbook each month:
11		Update the Settings for the current period
12		Export the 'SGA Data' memorized report from Quickbooks
13		Paste the data into the QBData sheet
14		Review that all test pass on the ErrorCk worksheet
15		Print the Report sheet to PDF and save to the P:/reports folder
16		
17	Assumptions	
18		The functions on the Report sheet assume that the QBData is pasted in row 1

Figure 62

SHEET NAMES SHORT BUT DESCRIPTIVE

Be sure that each worksheet has a short but descriptive name. Don't keep the default name (e.g., Sheet1, Sheet2).

Here are some examples of how I would and would not name worksheets:

I would use these names	I wouldn't use these names
Input	User Input Sheet
QBData	QuickBooks Data Export Worksheet
Report	Final Report For The Period
Bsheet	Balance Sheet At The End Of The Period

PREFER LOOKUPS TO DIRECT CELL REFERENCES

We haven't discussed Lookup functions yet, so if you are unfamiliar with them, this concept may not click at this time. However, I would still like to review this fundamental approach.

Often it is natural to use a cell reference (e.g., G12) to retrieve a value from another worksheet or cell. A cell reference may be used to pull the value from a cell or it may be used in a formula or as a function argument. In some cases, this approach is just fine.

However, it is generally better to use Lookup formulas in recurring-use workbooks. You see, workbooks used on a recurring basis often have data that shifts around each period and data sheets that may be refreshed with an import or copy/paste. Since the data may move around each period, a direct cell reference like G12 may break over time. Additionally, a direct cell reference may prevent you from creating consistent formulas if the order of the data doesn't match the order of your report. Thus, it is often better to use Lookup formulas to retrieve values from other sheets rather than direct cell references.

If you have played with Excel's Lookup functions, such as VLOOKUP, then this idea makes sense. If you haven't explored the power of Lookup functions, this concept will really click when we discuss various Excel Lookup functions.

XREF

Lookup functions are discussed in a subsequent book.

NO BLANK COLUMNS

In a data region, there is no need for blank columns between value columns. In other words, try to avoid inserting blank columns within your value or formula data regions.

I have seen many workbooks that include blank columns between data columns, and sometimes they are skinny. Typically, blank columns appear to be used for formatting purposes. However, there are other ways to achieve a similar printed output, such as using the Accounting format or by expanding the column width of the data columns. There may be times when the only way to achieve the specified printed output is to insert blank columns, but I would recommend that you leave data regions intact without inserting blank columns whenever possible, especially for recurring workbooks.

Blank columns can prevent the use of certain keyboard shortcuts, cause us to use overly complex formulas, prevent us from keeping our formulas consistent, prevent us from using certain advanced Excel features, and prevent us from easily updating all of the formulas within the range.

I've discovered that using this simple concept improves productivity.

CONSISTENT HEADERS

I've discovered that workbooks can more easily be maintained over time if headers and column labels are consistent between worksheets. For example, if the data sheet uses the three-letter month abbreviations (e.g., Jan, Feb, Mar), then your report sheet should also use the same three-letter abbreviations and should not use any other abbreviation or format to represent the period (e.g., 1,2,3; J, F, M; January, February, March). Keeping the column labels consistent between worksheets makes working with the workbook more efficient and automated.

When column labels represent time periods such as months, it is preferable to use actual dates rather than text labels for the column labels. By using an actual date, we enable the use of date-driven math and date functions, and generally have more flexibility. Plus, we can use custom date formatting to display the stored date value however we want.

Future detailed discussions about lookup functions will show the benefit of keeping labels and headers consistent between sheets.

As you work through the exercise workbooks during the remainder of this course, you'll notice that the design concepts discussed above are incorporated throughout.

EXAMPLES

Now, let's get some practical examples of the design concepts discussed this far.

PRACTICE

These concepts are illustrated in the Worksheet Organization.xlsx workbook.

NOTE

There are no hands-on exercises for this chapter. The sample workbook is provided to illustrate the concepts. There is not an answers version of the practice workbook.

Let's walk through each sheet, and I'll highlight certain items.

FLAT

We already discussed the benefits of having data in a flat format. So the referenced worksheet simply provides a sample.

PRACTICE

To see an illustration, please refer to the Flat worksheet.

As you can see, the flat file format has values populated for all rows and all columns. This makes it easy to use aggregation functions like SUMIFS and advanced features like PivotTables, filtering and sorting.

The data format on the bottom half of the sheet is more difficult to work with. We can't use SUMIFS, and we can't feed it into a PivotTable or use some of the other advanced features of Excel, such as filtering and sorting.

If we have a choice, we should elect to receive incoming data in a flat format since it will enable us to do our work more quickly.

CLEAN

Having clean data makes the data easier to work with, allowing us to use easy formulas.

PRACTICE

To see an illustration, please refer to the Clean worksheet.

For example, it would be relatively easy to aggregate and summarize the clean data. We could convert the range to a Table, use SUMIFS, drop it into a PivotTable, perform sorting and filtering, or use a number of other built-in features and functions to work with this clean data.

The bottom section represents data that is not clean; this format is not ideal. The blank columns and rows make it difficult to navigate and write structured formulas. It requires manual cleanup before the data can be fed into a PivotTable. Note that the SUM functions within the data region make it tough to compute a grand total of the Amount column without double counting. The subtotal row labels are the same as the data row labels, making it tough to use a SUMIFS function. We can't easily perform sorting and filtering on the range, and it's hard to use any of Excel's other advanced features on this range. The range has a header (the filter header) and a footer (printed date) that make the data more challenging to work with.

I hope that this worksheet drives home the point that the way the data is stored within a worksheet greatly impacts our ability to work with it and thus impacts our productivity.

UNIFORM

Uniform data is easier to work with. For purposes of our discussion, data is uniform when the report sheet and the data sheet both have the same orientation (horizontal or vertical).

PRACTICE

To see an illustration, please refer to the Uniform worksheet.

The top section illustrates uniform data. Both the report and the data store months in columns. That is, they both have the same horizontal orientation. You can see how easy it was to write a formula to tabulate the data.

The bottom section illustrates inconsistent formats. The report shows months in rows, but the data stores months in columns. The report has a vertical orientation, but the data has a horizontal orientation. As a result, you can see that we needed to use a complex formula to build the report. Complex formulas are more difficult to maintain and troubleshoot over time, especially when users' skill sets vary.

XREF

The functions used to compute the report on this sheet, including OFFSET and MATCH, are discussed in the lookups chapter in a subsequent book.

SPLIT

We discussed the benefits of splitting the data worksheet from the report worksheet.

PRACTICE

To see an illustration, please refer to the Split Report and Split Data worksheets.

Often, it is possible to place the data and the report on two different worksheets, especially when the report is a summary of the detail. When the report needs to include all of the transaction details, then you are better off keeping the report and the data sheets the same.

Splitting the sheets creates great efficiency for recurring workbooks because it is fast to update the report when you can simply paste the new data into the data sheet. Your smart formulas pull and summarize the data from the data sheet into the report sheet automatically. I call this type of setup hands-free reporting, because you just paste in the new data, and the formulas take over to pull the values into the report.

The example included has two sheets. One is Split Data, which represents the data that is pasted in each period, while the Split Report sheet pulls the values from the data sheet. This type of structure works well when the value labels are relatively static, and there aren't many new labels being added each month. If new labels are added each month, then a PivotTable would be a better approach since PivotTables automatically expand to include any new labels in the data source.

XREF

PivotTables are covered in a subsequent book.

SUBTOTALS OUTSIDE

Placing formulas, including subtotal formulas, outside of the data region is generally a good idea.

PRACTICE

To see an illustration, please refer to the Subtotals Outside worksheet.

Thus, in this example, you'll notice that the top section places the subtotals outside of the data region. This makes it easier to maintain the worksheet, move data around, navigate, update new data, and update formulas.

The bottom section illustrates subtotals that are embedded inside of data region. Sometimes we are required to produce reports in this exact format. However when this is not a strict requirement, it is generally a good idea to place formulas outside of data regions.

NOTE

The quarter subtotal formulas in the sample worksheet are outside of the data region, and that is good. However you'll notice that they use unique formulas for each column, and that does not conform to the formula consistency concept. Thus, the Extra Credit worksheet in the workbook shows formulas that conform to both concepts. Those advanced functions will be discussed at length in the Lookups chapter in a subsequent book.

SUBTOTALS ABOVE

In some cases it may be a good idea to place the summary formulas above the data region rather than below it. This would be the case when the report summary needs to be included on the same worksheet as the data, and the data is refreshed on a recurring basis with the number of data rows varying each period. If the summary formulas are positioned above the range, then in subsequent months you can just paste in the new data, and the formulas will automatically include the new data. If the summary formulas were under the data region, then updating the sheet is more time consuming, since you need to ensure that the formulas will be preserved.

PRACTICE

To see an illustration, please refer to the Subtotals Above worksheet.

Note that I intentionally placed the SUM formula in a different column than the Amount column. This was done so that I can use a column only reference (E:E) inside of the SUM function so that no matter how many rows next period's data occupies, all data rows will be included.

CONSISTENT

It is better to have consistent formulas in an area, rather than unique formulas for each cell, row, or column. Writing formulas that can be filled down and to the right and continue to work takes more time up front, but they are more efficient in recurring workbooks because they are easier to update.

PRACTICE

To see an illustration, please refer to the Consistent worksheet.

In the sample exercise, the top section represents the use of inconsistent formulas to retrieve values from the data into the report. They are simple cell references, and even though they are relative, you can't fill the formula down and to the right. You can fill the formula down through the Actual column, but you can't fill the formula to the right, meaning there are two formulas to update instead of one. To me this is a problem because it requires more effort to maintain the worksheet over time. Additionally, these formulas only happen to work because the data and report contain the same departments in the same order. If these departments were altered in any way, or placed in a different order, the formulas would be even more difficult to update. To me, it is better to take the time to write a clever formula that we can fill down through the Actual column AND fill right through the Budget column.

If you are familiar with the SUMIFS function, then the application of it in this context will make perfect sense. If you haven't yet explored the SUMIFS function, don't worry; we'll spend quite a bit of time on this remarkable function.

XREF

The SUMIFS function is discussed in a subsequent book.

COLUMN A

This concept simply states that we use Column A for labels only, and our data begins at Column B. I can't support this concept by stating that it drives productivity, efficiency, or accuracy; it is just a personal preference.

⏺ PRACTICE

To see an illustration, please refer to the Column A worksheet.

In my opinion, this practice makes worksheets cleaner and more organized, and I'm always happy to share my opinion, since it is one thing that I am an expert on!

The sample worksheet shows how all of the section labels are in Column A, and how the data doesn't begin until Column B.

CHAPTER CONCLUSION

Well my friend, these are my thoughts on how to best structure your worksheets. I hope that you find these concepts as useful and beneficial as I have. I have purposefully placed these concepts early in our overall series so that you'll be able to incorporate them into your workbooks.

Chapter 17: Nested Functions

Throughout the Excel University series, we'll work through many powerful worksheet functions. I want to be sure that we are on the same page with respect to functions, formulas, and nested functions.

SET UP

During our time together, I'll use the word function to describe a worksheet function, such as, SUBTOTAL or SUM. I'll use the word formula to describe the equation in a cell that is followed by an equal sign. The formula may contain operators (+, -), cell references, range references, named references, values, and functions. A formula may be something simple, such as:

```
=A1+B12
```

A formula may include a worksheet function:

```
=SUBTOTAL(9,A1:A10)
```

A formula may include multiple worksheet functions:

```
=SUBTOTAL(9,A1:A10)+SUM(G10:G20)
```

A formula may include a Named Reference:

```
=SUM(A10:A20)*commission_rate
```

> **XREF**
> Named References are discussed in Chapter 7.

So far, so good? Good. Now, earlier in this course we discussed functions and function arguments. Consider the PMT function, which computes the monthly payment of a loan. The PMT function has several arguments, such as the term and principal amount. Function arguments can be numerical values (10), cell references (A1), range references (A1:B10), or other functions.

I'll state that part again. *Function arguments can be other functions.*

When Excel evaluates a function, it begins by converting all of its arguments into values. So, for cell reference arguments, that means retrieving the value from the referenced cell. For arguments that are other functions, Excel first evaluates the function and then returns its result as the argument value. I'll refer to this concept as nested functions.

Let's play with this further, as it represents a fundamental concept needed to create powerful Excel formulas.

HOW TO

Mechanically setting up a nested function is simple. However, as you develop sophisticated formulas, nested functions can be conceptually daunting. Indeed, for some of my more advanced formulas, I sometimes use intermediate cells to form the building blocks of the final formula. Once each of the individual components is working properly, I'll combine them into a single formula.

However, for most day-to-day requirements, you'll find it's easy to nest functions both mechanically and conceptually once you get the hang of it.

For most basic formulas and functions, you could probably avoid using nested functions. This is because you could use intermediate helper cells to compute the arguments required and then pass the cell references to the main function. However, this approach generally results in worksheets that display more information than needed, namely, all of the intermediate helper formulas.

Let's start with some simple examples. Throughout the series, we will build upon this fundamental concept to achieve some remarkable formulas.

A function I use frequently is the ROUND function, which rounds a value to a specified number of decimals.

The syntax for the ROUND function:

```
=ROUND(number, num_digits)
```

Where:

- **number** is the number to round
- **num_digits** is the number of digits to which you want to round the number argument. For example, 2 would round to cents. 0 would round to whole dollars. Negative 3 (-3) would round to thousands.

Most frequently, I wrap the ROUND function around another function. To be clear, I typically use a function as the number argument of the ROUND function. This is a classic nested function situation, where one function represents the argument of another.

For example, I may use the ROUND function to round the results of a SUM function. Since I don't want to occupy two cells in the worksheet to accomplish this task, such as having one cell for the SUM function and the other cell for the ROUND function, I'll nest the functions and use the SUM function as the first argument of the ROUND function. For example:

=ROUND(SUM(A1:A10),0)

Where:

- **SUM(A1:A10)** is the value I want rounded
- **0** means that I want to round the value to the nearest whole number

When Excel computes the formula, the SUM function is evaluated first, and its result is passed into the ROUND function as its first argument.

EXAMPLES

OK, now let's work several examples together.

PRACTICE

To follow along, please refer to Nested Functions.xlsx.

VIDEO

To watch me complete the exercises, please visit the Excel University video library at www.clickconsulting.com/books.

BALANCE SHEET

In this example, you'll need to use the ROUND function in a balance sheet.

PRACTICE

To follow along, please refer to the Exercise 1 worksheet.

When you inspect the displayed value on the balance sheet, you'll notice that Total Assets is equal to $537,970. This agrees to Total Liabilities and Equity. But, when you look more closely, you'll see that Total Assets is actually $537,970.28 and Total Liabilities and Equity is $537,970.15. This results in a difference of $0.13.

By wrapping a ROUND function around the SUBTOTAL functions used to compute the totals, we can balance the balance sheet, resulting in a difference of $0.00. I know that in my life as accountant, statements that tie-out to the penny bring me great joy.

So, the first task will be to nest the SUBTOTAL functions inside of a ROUND function. For example, the new Total Assets formula is:

=ROUND(SUBTOTAL(9,C18:C21),0)

Where:

- **SUBTOTAL(9,C18:C21)** is the range of assets to total
- **0** tells the ROUND function to round the results of the SUBTOTAL function to the nearest whole dollar

Wrapping a ROUND function around the SUBTOTAL functions for Total Liabilities and Total Liabilities and Equity rounds these results to the nearest whole dollar. You will then observe that the difference goes to $0.00. Sweet!

COMMISSION SUMMARY

In this example, you'll need to use nested functions to compute a Total Commission amount rounded to two decimals.

PRACTICE

To follow along, please refer to the Exercise 2 worksheet.

In the Commissions section of the worksheet, you'll notice a SUM function computes the Total Sales. Then, you'll notice that Total Commission is computed by multiplying Total Sales by the Commission Rate. The result is a Total Commission amount of $6,229.4925. We would prefer that the Total Commission amount be rounded to the nearest penny, and thus decide to wrap a ROUND function around the Total Commission calculation.

The new Total Commission formula is:

```
=ROUND(C12*c_rate, 2)
```

Where:

- **C12*c_rate** is the commission amount (total sales times commission rate)
- **2** tells the ROUND function to round to two decimals

Generally, I'll wrap a ROUND function around most formulas that compute a dollar value through multiplication or division just to keep my dollar values rounded to pennies.

COMMISSION DETAIL

In this exercise, you'll be computing commission transactions rounded to the nearest cent.

PRACTICE

To follow along, please refer to the Exercise 3 worksheet.

In the Commissions section of the sheet, you'll notice that the current formula computes the commission amount for each transaction by multiplying the Amount by the Commission Rate. This results in commission amounts that extend beyond cents. Thus, we will wrap a ROUND function around the formula that computes the commission amount. The new Commission formula is:

```
=ROUND(C13*c_rate,2)
```

Where:

- **C13*c_rate** is the commission calculation
- **2** tells the ROUND function to round to two decimals

CHAPTER CONCLUSION

Nested functions represent one of the key concepts for building useful and powerful formulas in Excel. We'll certainly be using nested functions, lots of them actually, during our time together. By the end of this series, you will be a nested functions master!

Chapter 18: Selection Groups

While the concept of selection groups may be so obvious that everyone already knows about it, the goal of this first book is to ensure a common background, and thus I make no assumptions about what may or may not be common Excel knowledge. Therefore, let's discuss selection groups, so that I know we are all on the same page before we move along.

SET UP

If you are going to do the same task on many items, rather than perform that task one time for each item, you can often select all of the items and then perform the task. Generally it is faster to select all items and then perform the task just once.

This concept applies to cells, ranges, sheets, and other items. Not all tasks that can be performed on a single item can be performed on a selection group, but most of the basic tasks work fine.

Instinctively, when you need to apply the same cell format to many cells, you first select the group of cells and then apply the format to the group. You don't typically select each cell one at a time and then apply the cell format. This same concept can be applied in many different ways in Excel, so we'll simply expand upon this idea.

Let's see how.

HOW TO

Let's start at the beginning, with cells.

CELLS

If you want to format more than one cell, rather than format each cell individually, it is faster to first select the cells and then apply the formatting.

To select adjacent cells, simply select the first cell and then hold the mouse button down to drag to the last cell that you want to select. Now, anything you do is done to all of the cells at the same time.

> **KB**
>
> To select an adjacent range of cells with the keyboard, simply hold down the Shift key as you use the Arrow keys on your keyboard.

NONADJACENT CELLS

To select cells that are not adjacent, simply hold down the Ctrl key while selecting the individual cells with your mouse. Using this technique, you can select a mixture of ranges as well as individual cells.

> **KB**
>
> While there is a way to select nonadjacent cells with just the keyboard, I prefer to use the mouse because I think it is faster. If you want to explore how to select nonadjacent cells using the keyboard, the F8 key toggles you into Extend Selection mode, making this possible.

CELLS AND FORMULAS

If you select a group of cells, enter a formula (or a value), and then press Enter, the formula (or value) does not fill to all selected cells. If you want the formula or value that you enter to be filled to all selected cells, even if they are not adjacent, simply hold down the Ctrl key while you press Enter.

This works with both formulas and values.

> **KB**
>
> Hold Ctrl when you press the Enter key to fill the entry to all selected cells.

RANGES

You can select multiple ranges by holding down the Ctrl key while using the mouse to select each range.

SHEETS

You can also select a group of worksheets. If you select multiple sheets at the same time, any task you perform is applied to all of the sheets. This includes moving and deleting sheets and making any changes, such as cell formatting, cell value entries, and cell formula entries.

Remember to unselect the group after you are done, because as long as the group is selected, anything you do is done to all selected sheets.

There are certain restrictions to be aware of. For example, you can't turn on or off worksheet protection with a worksheet group.

> **XREF**
>
> If you need to turn on or off worksheet protection on lots of sheets, a macro is useful. Macros are discussed in a subsequent book.

To group adjacent sheets, click the first sheet tab and then hold down the Shift key on your keyboard and click the last sheet tab in the group.

To group nonadjacent sheets, hold down the Ctrl key on your keyboard and then individually click on each of the tabs in the group.

To ungroup sheets, click on any sheet outside of the group. If all sheets in the book are in the group, then simply click on any sheet tab.

> **KB**
>
> To group-select adjacent sheets, hold down the Shift key and then use Ctrl+PageUp/PageDown to navigate to the next/previous sheet. As you navigate to the next sheet, it is automatically added to the group. To ungroup, simply use Ctrl+PageUp/PageDown to navigate to a sheet outside of the group.

EXAMPLES

Let's get some hands-on experience with selection groups.

PRACTICE

To follow along, please refer to Selection Groups.xlsx.

VIDEO

To watch me complete the exercises, please visit the Excel University video library at www.clickconsulting.com/books.

CELLS

In this first exercise, you have a worksheet that requires the user to enter certain values. You want to highlight the input cells. Rather than apply the Input cell style to each input cell one at a time, you decide to select all of the input cells and then apply the style to the group.

PRACTICE

To follow along, please refer to the Exercise 1 worksheet.

XREF

The functions used in this example worksheet are VLOOKUP and EOMONTH. If you haven't explored these powerful worksheet functions yet, don't worry, you will. They are explored in detail in a subsequent book.

To group-select the input cells, simply click the first input cell and then hold down the Ctrl key on your keyboard. Next, use the mouse to select the other input cells. After all of the input cells are selected, simply apply the Input cell style.

XREF

The Input cell style is discussed in Chapter 14.

CELL FORMULAS

In this exercise, you'll write a formula and fill it down, all in one step.

PRACTICE

To follow along, please refer to the Exercise 2 worksheet.

First, highlight the range in the Total column where the formulas will be. Next, write the formula (a simple SUM function will suffice). Then, instead of pressing the Enter key on your keyboard, hold down the Ctrl key and then press Enter. You'll see that the formula was entered and filled down in a single step.

NOTE

In the real world, I occasionally use this technique when formulas are simple. More frequently, however, I write the formula and then use the double-click shortcut to fill it down. This is discussed in Chapter 6.

KB

The following is one sequence for performing this exercise with the keyboard only:

Navigate to the last row of the Total column. (It is an empty cell). You can do this by using a combination of Arrow keys and Ctrl+Arrow keys. Next, select cells upward by holding down Shift and Ctrl and then hitting the up Arrow. Then, unselect the header cell (Total label) by keeping the Shift key down, releasing the Ctrl key, and then hitting a single down Arrow. Write the formula. Remember that you can select function arguments with keyboard shortcuts, such as the Arrow key combinations previously discussed. After the formula is written, press Ctrl+Enter to fill the formula to the whole selected range. You may need to think about these steps now, but soon they'll become second nature.

RANGES

In this exercise, you'll implement Skinny Rows into a department report.

XREF

The Skinny Row Technique is discussed in Chapter 12.

PRACTICE

To follow along, please refer to the Exercise 3 worksheet.

Let's start by applying cell borders. Rather than applying borders one range at a time, we'll first select all ranges.

To select the ranges, simply highlight the range (the cells between the values and the subtotal formulas) for the first Group Subtotal and then hold down the Ctrl key and continue using your mouse to select the remaining ranges (the cells between the values and the subtotal formulas).

After all of the ranges are selected, apply a bottom cell border by using the button on the Home Ribbon tab.

A partial result is shown in Figure 63 below.

Figure 63

Now, let's make the rows skinny by changing the row height to 4 for all rows immediately above subtotals and the company total. You can change the row height when the entire row is selected or when any cell or cells in the row are selected. To be clear, you don't have to select the whole row to change the row height. So, if you still have the correct group of ranges selected, then just change the row height, and you are set. If not, you can select an entire row by clicking on the row number as an alternative. Hold down the Ctrl key and continue selecting the entire row for the remaining rows and then change the row height. If done correctly, each row in your selected group will now be a Skinny Row.

KB

The keyboard sequence for changing row height: Alt+O, R, E (f<u>o</u>rmat, <u>r</u>ow, h<u>e</u>ight).

SHEETS - EDIT

In this exercise, you'll select a group of sheets and make changes to them all at once.

PRACTICE

To follow along, please refer to the Exercise 4 worksheet.

We have three departments, and each department has its own sheet (E4 A, E4 B, and E4 C). After we set up each sheet, we noticed a typo. We noticed that total should be Total. Rather than update each sheet individually, we decide to select all three sheets and then make the change once.

NOTE

This assumes, of course, that total is found in the same cell on each sheet. That is, that the department sheets have an identical format.

Begin by selecting the group of department sheets. Then type Total into the cell that has the incorrect label total. Press Enter, and bam, you're done. That change has been made on all three sheets.

Next you need to write a function to compute the Total in each of the sheets. So again, rather than working sheet by sheet, you group-select the sheets and then write the function to compute the total.

SHEETS - DELETE

In this exercise, you'll delete multiple sheets all at once.

PRACTICE

To follow along, please refer to the Exercise 5 worksheet.

Since empty and unused sheets are a distraction and tend to waste time, you prefer to delete them. Rather than delete the unused sheets one at a time, you decide to group-select the sheets and then execute the delete command.

Start by selecting the extra sheets (Sheet1, Sheet2, and Sheet3). Next, delete them by using the following command:

- RibbonUI: Home > Delete Sheet
- MenuUI: Edit > Delete Sheet

Poof, gone!

KB

To delete a sheet (or group of sheets): Alt+E, L (sh__ee__t, de__l__ete).

CHAPTER CONCLUSION

Before you repeat a task many times on many different items, consider selecting the group of items first. It will probably save you some time.

Chapter 19: Workbook Design Principles

We come at long last to the final chapter of the Foundations book. I want to leave you with some guiding principles to keep in mind as you progress through this series and work on your own Excel workbooks.

As we proceed through the course, I'll refer back to these principles often so that you can see why we use specific features, functions, and techniques. As we explore Excel during our time together, we'll discover that we tend to select the functions and features that help us build our workbooks according to the following general design ideas:

1. Automation
2. Bulletproof
3. Check for Errors
4. Design
5. Efficiency

As it so happened, without much effort at all, these principles happen to begin with A, B, C, D and E. I didn't actually have to rename my original titles very much to get this to work. So, if it helps you remember them, terrific.

Let's dig in a little to better understand each of the design principles.

AUTOMATION

As I work in Excel, a question that is always on my mind is:

"How can I delegate this task to Excel?"

I try to maximize the use of Excel's features and functions to minimize the amount of manual labor required, even if it means spending more time up front to figure out a solution. If the process recurs, this set-up time is easily recaptured each subsequent period.

Two simple examples are (1) having Excel compute the last day of the month rather than having the user enter it and (2) having Excel automatically format cells based on their values rather than manually updating the formatting each period.

As you develop your workbooks, always ask the question, "How can I make Excel perform this task?" You'll quickly discover that Excel can perform many tasks that you have previously performed manually.

BULLETPROOF

As I work in Excel, another question always on my mind is:

"How can a user break my workbook?"

By anticipating how errors can occur and addressing them up-front, we build bulletproof workbooks that work reliably over time.

We've already discussed several specific features and functions that help us create workbooks that are more bulletproof. For example (1) using Data Validation to ensure users only enter data our formulas are designed to evaluate; (2) using Tables so that new data is included in our formulas; and (3) using the SUBTOTAL function so that new data is automatically included in the total.

As you build your workbooks, try to anticipate how errors can occur and then use Excel's features and functions to prevent those errors from occurring in the first place.

But what if despite all of your efforts to anticipate errors, an error does occur? You need to be able to have an efficient way to spot errors. That brings us to Error Checking.

CHECK FOR ERRORS

As I build my workbooks, I am always asking myself:

"How do I ensure that my work is accurate?"

In my opinion, it is the responsibility of the workbook administrator or the initial developer—not the user—to develop tests that monitor potential error conditions.

Assuming you are the workbook administrator, error checking is your responsibility; you create the formulas and therefore have the best understanding of how data flows through the workbook. You also have the best idea of how errors can occur and what to look for. You'll need to develop tests that look for error conditions, or at least potential error conditions, and report them to users so they have a chance to correct the errors. Your goal is to develop the most bulletproof workbooks, and even in the case where users figure out a way to break something, your error checking should be so comprehensive that users will know when errors occur and thus be able to correct them before finalizing their work.

An example of this technique is to build an Error Check worksheet or worksheets to provide a summary list of possible error conditions.

> **XREF**
>
> ErrorCk is discussed in Chapter 15.

DESIGN

Workbook and worksheet design and structure matter. Efficiency can be gained just by how you design and organize workbooks and worksheets.

Because we've covered these ideas at length in the Workbook Organization and Worksheet Organization chapters, we don't need to spend much time here.

Just keep in mind that design, structure, and organization matter and try to structure your workbooks and worksheets in such a way as to maximize efficiency.

> **XREF**
>
> Workbook Organization is discussed in Chapter 15.
>
> **XREF**
>
> Worksheet Organization is discussed in Chapter 16.

EFFICIENCY

While working in Excel, a question that is always on my mind is:

> *"How can I make this easy to maintain and update each cycle?"*

For workbooks used repetitively, such as every month or quarter, the goal is to make it fast and easy to update and maintain.

To be clear and for purposes of this course, improving efficiency means decreasing manual labor. Sometimes people refer to an efficient workbook as one that has the smallest file size. Sometimes efficiency is described as being the shortest possible formula or as a workbook whose formulas calculate the fastest.

For our purposes, we consider efficiency not in terms of computer efficiency, such as disk space or formula refresh time, but instead in terms of human time expended.

For us, improving efficiency means reducing human effort.

When given a choice between human processing time and computer processing time, we'll almost always use the Excel features, functions, and techniques that minimize human processing time at the expense of computer time and disk space. When deciding between two different approaches, we'll select the one that requires the least amount of manual time, even though it may result in a larger file, formulas that are more sophisticated, functions that are more complex, or longer computer processing.

Our notion of efficiency now has many Excel implications, and as we proceed together, we'll frequently refer back to efficiency. Following are a few general ideas to consider at this point.

MINIMIZE INPUT CELLS

As you create workbooks, try to minimize the number of input cells by maximizing the number of formula cells. That is, if Excel can compute a value, take the time to figure out the formula so that you don't need to manually key it in each period.

BEAUTIFUL FORMULAS

Try to write beautiful formulas. Can a formula be beautiful? Yes, I have seen many formulas that I consider beautiful. Then again, I'm an Excel nerd.

Following are some characteristics of beautiful formulas:

First, beautiful formulas are consistent throughout a region. That is, they are the same in a region and can be updated by simply modifying the upper-left formula in an area. These formulas will continue to work when filled down and to the right.

Next, beautiful formulas can accommodate minor structural changes, such as, when new rows of data are added or inserted. The SUBTOTAL function is one such function.

Beautiful formulas are rugged and can survive many cycles of use. For this reason, beautiful formulas tend to use Lookup functions rather than cell references. Even when the order of items is different between sheets, Lookup functions will work perfectly. Lookup formulas also perform well when pulling values from a data sheet into a report sheet.

ONE PLACE

Try to create control points. A control point is one place in the workbook where a single update can trigger many updates.

A simple example of this is placing the company name on a Start Here sheet. Then, throughout the remainder of the worksheets, you can retrieve the company name by pulling the value from the Start Here sheet. By changing the company name in one place on the Start Here sheet, you essentially push this updated value to all of the worksheets. If you are involved in closing the books, you could store the closing date in one sheet and then reference it throughout the workbook. This same concept applies to centrally storing constants, assumptions, headers, and settings.

Another example is the use of Styles. You can change the Style definition, and all cells that use that Style are updated.

So, breaking this down into a general idea, if a value appears frequently throughout the workbook, you can set up a control point so that the value can be updated throughout the workbook by changing a single cell value.

EFFICIENT USE

Besides developing Excel workbooks that are internally efficient, you need to interact with Excel efficiently. A fantastic way to do this is to use keyboard shortcuts. The more rapidly you can communicate with Excel, the more efficient you will be.

CHAPTER CONCLUSION

These are the basic concepts and principles that I use when I develop my real life workbooks. These ideas have helped guide me as I consider various features, functions, and approaches. I hope that they'll be as useful for you.

Conclusion

And that, my friend, concludes the Foundations book. My goal was to have this book steer us all to the same starting point. I hope that the prerequisites we've covered now enable us to build upon this foundation. We are now prepared for the features and functions that await us in the next book. I hope you'll decide to continue to the next step in our adventure together, and remember, Excel rules.

Printed in Germany
by Amazon Distribution
GmbH, Leipzig